COOKING WITH TRADER JOE'S

COOKBOOK

PACK A LUNCH

CÉLINE COSSOU-BORDES

Photographs by Tia Black

Cooking with Trader Joe's Cookbook: Pack a Lunch!
by Céline Cossou-Bordes
Photographs by Tia Black
Designed by Lilla Hangay
Produced by Deana Gunn and Wona Miniati

Published by Brown Bag Publishers, LLC
P.O. Box 235065
Encinitas, CA 92023

Printed in Korea through Overseas Printing Corporation

Library of Congress Cataloging-in-Publication Data
Cossou-Bordes, Céline.
Cooking with Trader Joe's Cookbook: Pack a Lunch!/
by Céline Cossou-Bordes; photographs by Tia Black – 1st ed.
Includes index.

I. Quick and easy cookery. 2. Trader Joe's (Store) I. Title.

ISBN   978-0-9799384-5-0   0-9799384-5-7

This book is an independent work not sponsored by or affiliated with Trader Joe's. Trader Joe's is a registered trademark of Trader Joe's Company.

Contents

Thank You Notes

Without a doubt, if Deana Gunn and Wona Miniati had not suggested a cookbook to me, I might never have dared. I thank them for making this amazing journey a reality.

To Tia Black for her beautiful photography, kindness, and professionalism. It has been wonderful working with you.

To my enthusiastic taste-testers and friends: Michael and Jackie Williams, Tia Black, Catie Grace Eyer, Kumi Lukes, Danielle Baum, Emily Henderson, Joanie Caicco, and Mary Ann Murray.

I'm grateful to the local community centers, where I teach my cooking classes, and their gracious staff. The Murrieta Community Center is where I started my journey as a cooking instructor in 2007. I am still there today, teaching popular "Cooking with Trader Joe's" cooking classes!

To Sylvain for taking such good care of my kids and my house while I was working and cooking.

To Tommy, Zoë, Lyla, Eva, and Audrey for being such great and fun models.

To my little artists, Tommy and Zoë, for their amazing drawings used in this book.

To my creative designer, Lilla Hangay, for bringing my recipes to life in such a lovely format.

To David Sullivan for lending his expert eye to edit and polish my manuscript.

To Eddy Kim for efficiently and accurately evaluating these recipes for nutritional data.

To Trader Joe's stores for promoting such an extensive, exotic, and unique selection of healthy meals and ingredients, which have provided much of the inspiration for this book.

Finally to my parents: my mother Josette, thank you for feeding me so well as I was growing up and being my first inspiration; my father Jean-Claude, thank you for introducing me to the finest ingredients by growing delicious vegetables and bringing home freshly caught fish.

This book is dedicated to Joël, Tommy, and Zoë, who have been through everything with me.

Introduction

Born in Paris and raised in the South of France, I discovered cooking as a child through my mother, who inherited her talents and recipes from a long family tradition of fine cooking.

When I was pregnant with my twins, I found myself surrounded by nannies, babysitters, new moms, and moms-to-be who had absolutely no clue how to feed and cook for their kids and families. I wasn't sure if I could do it either, given my already busy lifestyle, which was about to get even busier with the arrival of twins. I wanted my kids to eat healthy, organic homemade foods, and at the same time, I didn't want to slave in the kitchen after an exhausting day at work.

I know that some people didn't take my lofty goals seriously, thinking I had chosen a complicated and unrealistic way to feed my family. However, once I began to combine smart shortcuts with my simple European traditions, it became practical and (dare I say) easy to make and enjoy gourmet meals all week long. Trader Joe's became my new best friend. I began to share my recipes and secrets with other moms who were thrilled at the prospect of eating healthy and conveniently.

In 2007, I decided to create Celine's Cuisine (**www.celinescuisine.com**), a company specializing in healthy cooking education. To this day, I teach private cooking classes for adults, teenagers, and children, as well as group cooking classes at various local Inland Valley/San Diego community centers. I thrive on giving parents useful ideas and recipes for healthy, organic meals, and I share their satisfaction and passion in providing the best for their kids as well as themselves!

Why Pack A Lunch?

The concept of a packed lunch is nothing new. Lunchboxes have been extremely popular for a long time in many other countries, where they are part of the lunch culture. They are called bento in Japan, tiffin in India, dosirak in Korea, or baon in the Philippines. In the Western World, the concept has been reborn and is growing far beyond a humble PB&J sandwich and apple tucked in a brown paper bag.

All the recipes in this book create meals that are portable – they are easy to pack and travel well. The meals are perfect for lunch at work or school, on a picnic, while camping, on road or plane trips, or for a potluck. The benefits of a packed lunch include eating foods you really like, eating healthier, saving money, saving time, making it easy to diet or watch nutritional intake, and being more eco-friendly.

For many people, lunch food is often synonymous with take-out and fast food, such as burgers, pizza, and chicken nuggets. Although these foods are usually cheap, convenient, and well adapted to work and school environments, most have been linked to chronic diseases and long-term sicknesses, including diabetes, obesity, and cardiovascular problems.

The resurgence of interest in the packed lunch shows that we're all listening and making better choices. Years ago, it wasn't popular to "brown bag" a lunch, but now we look enviously at the person with homemade leftovers or carefully arranged Bento boxes from home. Instead of spending precious lunch breaks driving around town and waiting in lines, only to consume an unhealthy and high-calorie meal, many people are now taking their lunch to work. Whether you're watching your waist, your wallet, or the clock, a packed lunch has benefits on all levels.

The trend carries over to kids' lunches as well. Unhealthy cafeteria school lunches have been at the center of criticism and controversy these last few years. More and more parents are looking for healthy, balanced foods to pack without spending an hour every morning doing so. My kids love taking their lunch to school, and are proud to sit with their friends and open their lunchboxes. There is no need to wait in line and no despair at discovering they don't like the food being served. To my relief and satisfaction, my kids report back that they prefer their lunches to the burgers and pizza at the cafeteria – and their friends are asking their moms for a packed lunch, too! Who would have guessed?

This book has been designed with everyone in mind: the parent who packs lunches for the kids; the full-time working parent who needs to pack lunches for the entire family; the busy professional who cooks dinner and takes leftovers to work the next day and is desperate for new lunch ideas; the student who has only a few minutes to cook and needs to stick to a tight budget; the person who is vegetarian, gluten-free, or has other special diet needs; and anyone who wants to stop eating unhealthy fast-food lunches, save money, eat healthy, or lose weight.

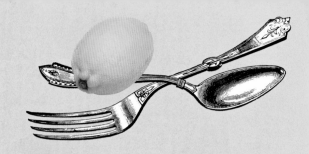

Chapter 1

Lunchbox Essentials

Are you overwhelmed at the thought of packing lunch for yourself or your family? This chapter contains my best lunchbox tips and recommended essentials. Given the right containers, a little organization, and Trader Joe's help, you will be packing healthy lunches in no time. Whether your goal is to eat healthy, save money, lose weight, or simply enjoy delicious gourmet food no matter where you are, this chapter will get you off to a running start.

Useful Tips

1. Pre-pack lunches when possible
When you pack the leftovers from dinner directly into your lunch container, the next day's lunch is already done. Simple twists on old favorites can inject fresh interest, such as cutting a leftover frittata with cookie cutters or placing fruits on a skewer.

2. Befriend ready-made foods
Use canned and frozen foods to speed lunch preparation. Canned legumes can become an express salad, and frozen vegetables can go into pasta or quiches. Many dishes such as soup, rice, and vegetables can be made in advance, frozen, and then thawed as needed.

3. Boost flavor with pre-made condiments
Stock your pantry and fridge with sauces, dips, salsas, and chutneys that can be added to simple pastas, sandwiches, and salads. These condiments can be either homemade or store-bought. Examples to consider are Tzatziki sauce, barbeque sauce, teriyaki sauce, curry, hummus, ranch dressing, and ketchup.

4. Mix textures, flavors, shapes, and colors
Include a variety of textures in a lunchbox – for example, serve crunchy veggies with soft applesauce. Use cookie cutters to create interesting shapes out of bread or cheese slices; small specialty cutters can be used to cut small shapes out of vegetable or fruit slices. Expand palates by playing with salty, sweet, spicy, and fruity flavors to make eating a real culinary adventure.

5. Organize
Keep a designated shelf in the fridge and pantry for lunch and snack items so you can quickly grab, pack, and go. Keep lunch containers in a specific drawer or cabinet, so that you aren't frantically searching for a particular box or lid in the morning.

6. Freeze

Freeze juice boxes, yogurt, or homemade smoothies. They will keep other foods cool and will thaw to just the right temperature and consistency by lunchtime.

7. Use yogurt

Yogurt is a universal favorite. Ever versatile, yogurt can be used as a dressing or dip, in smoothies, or in parfaits, layered with fruits, nuts, and cereals. If using flavored yogurts, beware brands which contain high amounts of sugar.

8. Think beyond mayonnaise

There are many healthy and interesting alternatives to classic mayo. Examples include hummus, Boursin cheese, The Laughing Cow spreadable cheese wedges, wasabi mayonnaise, cream cheese, tapenade, pesto, guacamole, ranch dressing, and salsa.

9. Keep vinaigrette handy

Pre-made or store-bought vinaigrette, doled out into a leak-proof container, will make it possible to assemble a delicious lunchbox in just minutes. Use the vinaigrette for salads, to flavor pasta, or as a dip.

10. Count the ways

A healthy lunchbox has 7 main components:

1. *Whole grain carbohydrates* – rice, noodles, crackers, pretzels, bread, pasta, etc.

2. *Protein* – tofu, eggs, chicken, turkey, fish, ham, etc.

3. *Whole fruit* (not fruit juice, fruit snacks, or fruit rolls) – grapes, tomatoes, apples, etc.

4. *Vegetable* – peas, carrots, broccoli, edamame, etc.

5. *Water* – pack in kid-friendly containers such as Sigg or Klean Kanteen.

6. *Dairy* – cheese, yogurt, etc.

7. *Love* – food made with love and care always tastes better.

Pack a Lunch with Trader Joe's

One of the biggest challenges in creating healthy lunchboxes is maintaining creativity and adding sufficient diversity to meals, all in a reasonable amount of time.

Thankfully, there is Trader Joe's. They offer a huge diversity of high-quality, delicious, healthy, and organic products, ranging from simple basics to hard-to-find exotic ingredients to healthy frozen foods and fully-prepared meals. It truly is possible to rely on Trader Joe's as your single source for all grocery needs. Additionally, because of their small store size and helpful crew, Trader Joe's is well adapted to easy and fast shopping – provided you find a parking spot!

For people who have a little more spare time and have access, I highly recommend buying fruits and vegetables from organic farms or your local food market.

Plan Ahead

There's a surefire way to make a painful chore out of packing lunches: start thinking about it 10 minutes before you're scheduled to leave the house. Just a little bit of planning can take the panic and desperation out of packing a lunch at the last minute. You might even catch yourself having fun!

I buy everything on weekends in order to have all ingredients ready and fresh on Sunday night for the rest of the week. I prepare or pre-pack nearly everything the night before. Bread, vegetables, fruits, or cheese are cut up ahead of time. Muffins, savory breads, cookies, mini tarts, crepes, and pancakes are baked and cooled ahead of time. Any sandwich fillings (egg, tuna, tofu, chicken salad) are mixed the night before and stored in the fridge. Canned fruit, yogurt, cheese, sauce, hummus, and chutney are portioned into small containers. Doing all this prep the night before makes morning lunchbox assembly a breeze. I like to make kids' lunches fun by adding a mini toy, a colorful sticker, or a handwritten note that says, "I love you and I'm thinking about you today!" Who knows, some adults might appreciate this gesture, too.

Choosing Containers and Lunchboxes

There are so many options for lunch containers; it's easy to feel overwhelmed. I've simplified the options below within two categories: carrying cases and food containers. Choose the combination you like best, or keep multiple options on hand to choose from, like I do. This way, I can opt for hot meals or cold meals, and we don't have the same thing every day for lunch.

Most schools don't make refrigerators available to children. To avoid spoilage of food that needs to stay refrigerated, you will need an insulated lunchbox and a Thermos or containers paired with an ice pack. Most of the kid-friendly lunches in this cookbook are eaten cool (i.e., packed in insulated lunchboxes with ice packs) or at room temperature. The only foods that are eaten warm are those packed in Thermoses or thermal food jars. To prevent illness-causing bacteria from growing in foods that must be kept cold or hot, make sure that the storage range is below 40°F or above 140°F.

On another safety note, some schools do not permit nuts and nut products to be brought in lunchboxes due to nut allergies. Check with your school before including nut products.

I advocate using reusable containers as much as possible, rather than disposable plastic bags, juice boxes, or plastic utensils that get tossed into landfills. Eco-friendly options for the various components of a lunchbox are highlighted below.

1. Carrying cases. While most lunchboxes don't come in direct contact with food, they are in daily contact with hands and must also be made of safe materials. Cotton, bamboo, and stainless steel, are usually safe materials for lunchboxes. If using plastic or vinyl lunchboxes, make sure that they are labeled free of lead, phthalates, and BPA. Regardless of the type of lunchbox, look for ones that are sturdy, easy to clean, and easy for children to open.

a) Insulated lunchbox/bag. If no refrigerator or microwave is available at work or school, invest in insulated lunchboxes. Paired with Thermoses or ice packs, an insulated lunchbox can keep hot foods hot and cold foods cold for hours.

b) Non-insulated lunchbox. This option is fine for foods that can remain at room temperature for several hours.

2. Food containers. For the safest lunches possible, choose components made of harmless materials. Plastic containers, while convenient and light, require careful selection – look for ones that are labeled phthalate-free and BPA-free. Avoid plastics #3, #6, and #7, which have contaminants, leach chemicals, and are in general unsafe for food. To check the type of plastic, look on the bottom of the container within the recycle triangle symbol. Metal containers and Thermoses are other good options.

a) Thermos/thermal food jar. A stainless steel Thermos or thermal food jar (wide-mouth, stackable containers) safely keeps foods hot for up to 6 hours, or cold up to 3 hours. Wide-mouth thermoses work well for one-dish meals such as stews, pastas, and soups. For kids, there are many character designs to choose from, including Superman, Tinker Bell, or Dora the Explorer. For optimum results, it's best to pre-heat or pre-chill a Thermos before adding food. To pre-heat, fill the thermos with hot water, let it stand for a minute or two, empty, and fill with hot food, closing the lid immediately. To pre-chill, fill with ice water for 1 to 2 minutes, discard water, and fill with chilled lunches.

b) Plastic or glass containers. In recent years, lunch-size containers with easy snap-on lids have become very popular. These containers can keep your food at room temperature or cold when packed with an ice pack. If you have access to a microwave, you can reheat your food in these containers.

c) Bento box. The classic bento box, a Japanese creation, has divided compartments meant to house various foods in one container. Most Japanese bento boxes are not microwave safe, since the typical Japanese bento is eaten at room temperature. When choosing a bento system, look for containers that are leak proof and easy to wash and maintain.

3. Extras

a) Water bottles. Re-usable water bottles instead of juice boxes and disposable water bottles are better for our planet.

b) Ice packs. Non-toxic, lunchbox-size plastic ice packs are available in a variety of designs at superstores such as Target. You may also use flexible ice blankets, a quilt of small reusable ice packs. Ice blankets can be cut apart to produce many small ice packs, perfect for throwing into an insulated lunch bag.

c) Food wrap. Sometimes you may want to wrap sandwiches tightly instead of placing them in containers. Safe packaging options include butcher paper and soy-based (i.e., not petroleum-based) waxed paper bags. For snacks, I love fabric bags, handmade or store-bought, that come in pretty colors and designs. They're simple to wash and keep food fresh all day. Many local farmers markets are starting to carry reusable fabric snack bags.

d) Silverware. Real silverware and cloth napkins add a classy touch, in addition to being environmentally friendly. Make your daily lunch a joyous occasion, even if it's in a lunchbox.

Shopping Resources

Superstores such as Target have a good selection of many of the lunch carrying products we've discussed: thermal food jars for kids and adults, insulated and non-insulated lunchboxes, reusable water bottles, etc. An online search will yield additional varieties of lunch containers, including large thermal lunch jars with multiple containers inside. Ice blankets are widely available at sporting stores, wholesale food stores, and drugstores. Online resources include:

Amazon: the biggest online mega-store – **www.amazon.com**
Thermos: insulated water bottles, food jars, and lunch bags –
www.thermos.com
Eco Lunchbox: stainless steel lunchboxes and cotton bags –
www.ecolunchboxes.com
Go Green Lunchbox: stylish and convenient lunchboxes –
www.gogreenlunchbox.com
Kids Konserve: full line of eco-friendly lunch kits with metal dishes –
www.kidskonserve.com
Lunch Bots: metal containers – **www.lunchbots.com**
Laptop Lunches: safe plastic bento boxes – **www.laptoplunches.com**
Planet Box: metal bento trays – **www.planetbox.com**
Citizen Pip: full line of eco-friendly plastic lunch kits with snap lids –
www.citizenpip.com
Tupperware: full line of plastic containers – **www.tupperware.com**

Kitchen Staples

Stock your kitchen with strategic basics, and you will have the foundation to create meals quickly. Below are the kitchen staples I like to keep on hand, as well as a list of my favorite kitchen equipment.

Pantry

Extra virgin olive oil
Balsamic or your favorite vinegar
Vegetable, chicken, or beef broth
   (available in 32-oz cartons)
Salsa
Soyaki (teriyaki sauce) or soy sauce
Olives, marinated artichokes, artichokes
   hearts, or roasted red peppers
Pasta, rice, or couscous
Sun dried tomatoes
Canned beans
Canned tomatoes
Bruschetta, tapenade, or chutney
Peanut butter, almond butter, or other nut butter
Nuts (these can be stored in the freezer if they are not used quickly)
Dressing

Freezer

Frozen brown rice or jasmine rice (packaged as 2-cup pouches in a box)
Frozen pie crust and artisan puff pastry (2 sheets per package)
Frozen crushed garlic (packaged as frozen cubes)
Frozen mangoes, berries, or other frozen fruit
Frozen vegetables such as broccoli, peas, spinach, and green beans
Chicken, beef, fish, shrimp, or scallops. Chicken, salmon, and steaks
   are often sold in separately packaged freezer-safe bags, or you can
   separate them into individual portions before freezing.
Frozen boxed appetizers for unexpected guests
Frozen French toast or waffles for rushed mornings
Plain or chocolate croissants for lazy Sunday mornings
Pita bread, bagels, English muffins or other breads
Pre-made meals such as frozen risotto or Mandarin orange chicken
   (great with frozen brown rice or vegetable fried rice)
Amazing pre-made frozen desserts: lava chocolate cake, raspberry or
   blueberry tarts, and cheesecake

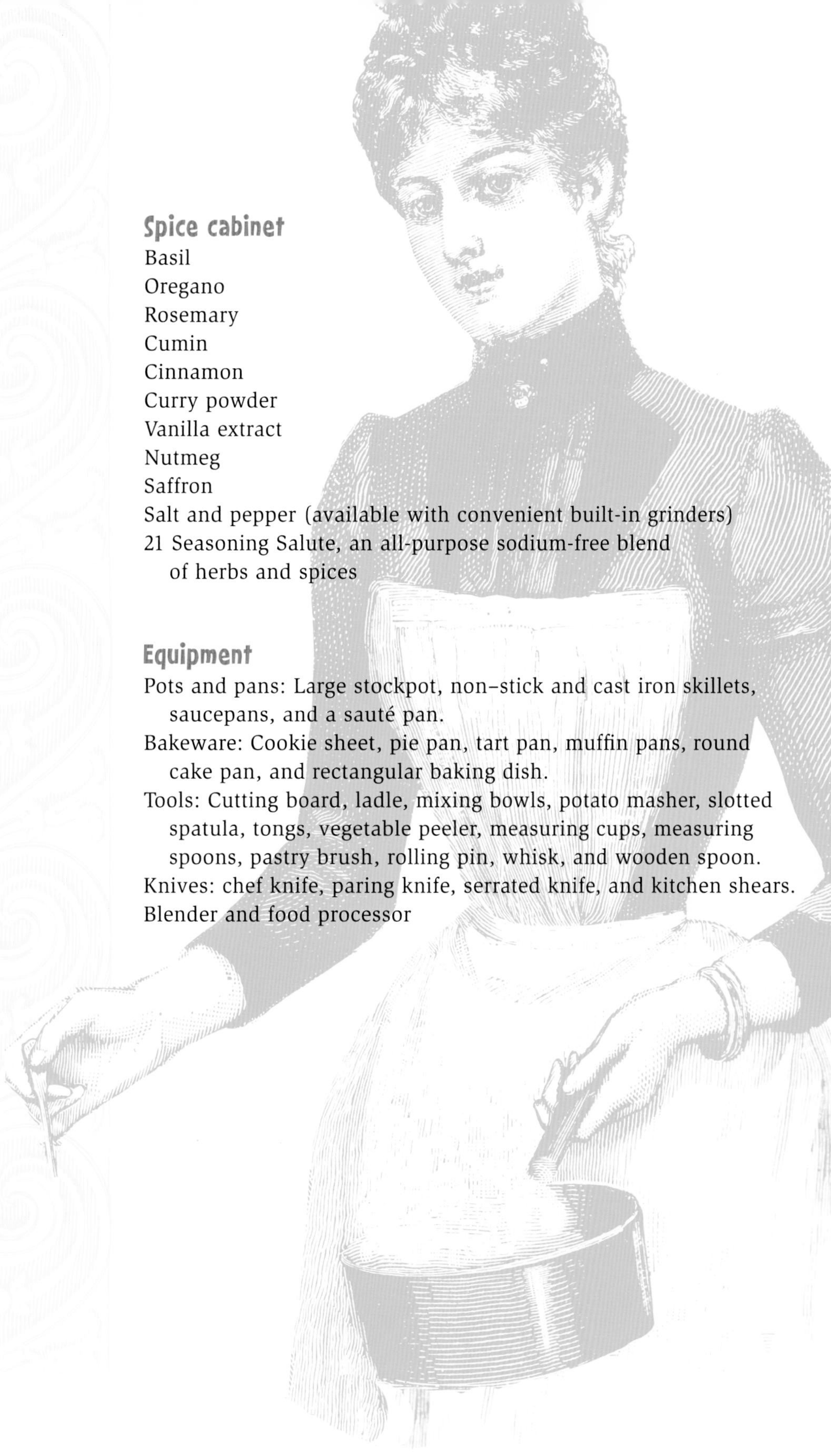

Spice cabinet

Basil
Oregano
Rosemary
Cumin
Cinnamon
Curry powder
Vanilla extract
Nutmeg
Saffron
Salt and pepper (available with convenient built-in grinders)
21 Seasoning Salute, an all-purpose sodium-free blend
   of herbs and spices

Equipment

Pots and pans: Large stockpot, non–stick and cast iron skillets,
   saucepans, and a sauté pan.
Bakeware: Cookie sheet, pie pan, tart pan, muffin pans, round
   cake pan, and rectangular baking dish.
Tools: Cutting board, ladle, mixing bowls, potato masher, slotted
   spatula, tongs, vegetable peeler, measuring cups, measuring
   spoons, pastry brush, rolling pin, whisk, and wooden spoon.
Knives: chef knife, paring knife, serrated knife, and kitchen shears.
Blender and food processor

About the Recipes

Each recipe in this book contains ingredients that can be found at Trader Joe's. While many of the ingredients are generic, ingredients that are capitalized and written in bold typeface are specific products found at Trader Joe's.

Each recipe includes prep time and cooking time. For those dishes that are assembled and then simmer on the stove or bake in the oven, I indicate "hands-off cooking time." Take this time to relax or catch up on other work.

Each recipe contains nutritional data. Optional ingredients are not included when calculating nutritional data. Serving sizes follow FDA guidelines and dietitian recommendations.

Each recipe contains indicators for recipes that are

gluten-free   **vegetarian**   **kid-friendly**

Please note that the FDA has not established a standard to define the term gluten-free. Products at Trader Joe's may be labeled "no gluten ingredients used" which does not necessarily exclude the chance of cross-contamination if it is produced in a facility that handles gluten products. Persons with celiac disease or severe gluten allergies should note that unless a product is labeled and tested gluten-free by standards such as ELISA and produced in a dedicated facility, there is possibility of cross-contamination.

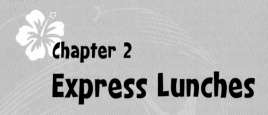

Chapter 2
Express Lunches

Salads

Greens with Pears, Grapes, and Candied Pecans

The quintessential salad! Packed with nutrients and vitamins, this salad artfully combines flavors and textures – sweet and sour, soft and crispy, dry and juicy. If that isn't enough, add crumbled goat cheese for extra depth of flavor. Amazingly delicious and healthy, it will make you feel good when you make it, and even better when you savor it.

2 pieces jarred **Pear Halves in White Grape Juice**, drained and diced

½ cup **red grapes**, halved

¼ cup **Candied Pecans**

½ (5-oz) bag **Organic Baby Spring Mix** or other salad greens

<u>*Vinaigrette*</u>

1 Tbsp white balsamic vinegar

1 tsp lemon juice

½ Tbsp honey

2 Tbsp extra virgin olive oil

⅛ tsp salt

Pinch black pepper

Prep time 10 minutes

Serves 2

1 In a small bowl, whisk vinaigrette ingredients. Pour in a container and refrigerate.

2 In another container, toss pears and grapes and then sprinkle with pecans. Top with salad leaves. Cover (without mixing in salad leaves) and place in fridge until ready to eat.

3 Remove salad and dressing from fridge 10 minutes before serving. Just before eating, place salad in a large cup or bowl and pour dressing on top. Mix gently.

Nutrition Snapshot

Per serving: 336 calories, 16g fat, 2g saturated fat, 2g protein, 35g carbs, 3g fiber, 25g sugar, 241mg sodium

Endive, Blue Cheese, Apple, and Walnut Salad

A French classic! Endive is a fantastic winter vegetable. Very refreshing, crunchy and juicy, you can eat it steamed, braised, or just raw like in this salad. Full of fiber and made of 90% water, this vegetable is your best friend if you want to lose weight. The flavor and texture of endive, blue cheese (Roquefort), and walnuts pair well, making this one of my favorite winter salads. I added fresh apple to this recipe, but fresh pear works just as well. Do not forget to discard the hearts (end core) of the endive to avoid their bitterness.

3 medium-size Belgian endive heads

1 Granny Smith apple, peeled, cored and cut into ½-inch pieces

1 tsp lemon juice

2 oz blue cheese or Roquefort cheese, crumbled

¼ cup chopped raw walnuts

Mustard Vinaigrette

1 Tbsp white balsamic vinegar

1 tsp Dijon mustard

2 Tbsp olive oil

Salt and pepper to taste

Prep time 10 minutes

Serves 2

Vegetarian Gluten Free

1 In a small bowl, whisk vinaigrette ingredients. Pour into a container and refrigerate.

2 Wash, core, and thinly slice endive heads, discarding endive hearts. Place in a bowl. Add chopped apple. Sprinkle with lemon juice, tossing to coat. Add cheese and walnuts.

3 Pour vinaigrette over salad and toss just before serving.

Nutrition Snapshot

Per serving: 378 calories, 32g fat, 8g saturated fat, 9g protein, 19g carbs, 4g fiber, 10g sugar, 576mg sodium

At the Heart of Avocado Salad

This exotic, colorful, and light salad is perfect for a hot summer lunch. It is easy and quick to make, using only a few ingredients from the pantry and the fridge. I always keep marinated artichoke hearts and palm hearts in my pantry – they are splendid ingredients for a classy salad. Omit the prosciutto for a great vegetarian salad.

2 small avocados

1 tsp lemon juice

1 (12-oz) jar **Marinated Artichoke Hearts**, drained and chopped

1 (12-oz) jar **Palm Hearts**, drained and chopped

3 pearl or Roma tomatoes, cut in wedges

4 slices prosciutto, cut in 1-inch pieces

8 black olives, chopped

¼ cup chopped fresh cilantro

Vinaigrette

1 Tbsp white balsamic vinegar

1 tsp lemon juice

2 Tbsp olive oil

Salt and pepper to taste

Prep time 10 minutes

Serves 4

  *Omit prosciutto

1   In a small bowl, whisk vinaigrette ingredients.

2   Peel and cut avocados into bite-size pieces and drizzle with lemon juice.

3   In a medium bowl, mix avocado, artichoke hearts, palm hearts, tomato, prosciutto, olives, and cilantro.

4   When ready to eat, pour vinaigrette over salad and toss.

Nutrition Snapshot

Per serving: 320 calories, 28g fat, 4g saturated fat, 8g protein, 13g carbs, 8g fiber, 1g sugar, 714mg sodium

Creamy Carrot Salad

When I was a kid, my mother would serve carrottes râpées *(grated carrots), an important appetizer that is part of the French diet and can be found everywhere, including bistros, restaurants, and cafeterias. I never liked it, until one day when she added raisins and transformed the salad into a delicious and sweet dish. I still make it this way, but now I also add peaches and yogurt for additional substance. This velvety and delicious salad is ideal during hot summers.*

1 cup **Shredded Carrots**

2 Tbsp golden raisins

3 pieces jarred **Peach Halves in White Grape Juice**, drained and diced

2 Tbsp pine nuts

1 Tbsp **Pomegranate Seeds**

1 cup plain whole milk yogurt, such as **Plain Cream Line Yogurt**

½ tsp **21 Seasoning Salute** spice blend, or your favorite seasoning

2 Tbsp chopped cilantro

¼ tsp salt

Pinch black pepper

Prep time 10 minutes
Serves 3

1 In a medium bowl, mix carrots, raisins, peaches, pine nuts, pomegranate seeds, and yogurt.

2 Stir in seasoning, cilantro, salt and pepper.

Nutrition Snapshot
Per serving: 235 calories, 7g fat, 3g saturated fat, 5g protein, 43g carbs, 5g fiber, 37g sugar, 273mg sodium

Moroccan-Style Orange Salad

As in Morocco, oranges grow in almost every backyard in Southern California, and they are just as delicious. I particularly like the idea of adding oranges to salads, where the vinaigrette balances their sweetness and enhances their flavor. This exotic and refreshing salad shines with the Moroccan flavors of cinnamon, honey, and mint.

3 navel or Valencia oranges

3 Tbsp olive oil

Juice of ½ orange

Juice of ½ lemon

¼ tsp ground cinnamon

1 Tbsp honey

12 **Pitted Kalamata Olives**

1 avocado

½ small red or white onion, thinly sliced

1 Tbsp toasted pine nuts

Salt and pepper to taste

⅓ cup chopped fresh mint

Prep time 10 minutes

Serves 3

1 Cut top and bottom ends off oranges. Using a sharp knife, peel rind along with outer layer of skin, exposing pulp. Cut each orange into 8 wheels. Reserve juice and set aside.

2 Whisk olive oil, orange and lemon juices, cinnamon, and honey in a salad bowl. Add oranges, olives, avocado, onion, and pine nuts; mix with large spoon. Adjust seasonings with salt and pepper as needed.

3 Garnish with mint and drizzle with more olive oil. Serve cold or at room temperature.

Nutrition Snapshot

Per serving: 342 calories, 54g fat, 4g saturated fat, 2g protein, 38g carbs, 8g fiber, 22g sugar, 226mg sodium

Chapter 2
Express Lunches

Smoothies

Berrylicious Fruit Smoothie

Smoothies are yummy, versatile, and an antioxidant-rich addition to any lunch, snack, or even breakfast. Kept refrigerated, they stay fresh and delicious for all day long. My 6-year-old daughter created this recipe. She had read a story about a little girl making a smoothie and decided to create her own. She wanted to create a pink smoothie before any other consideration, and it came out so well that I decided to include it here. Thank you, little Zoë.

1 cup yogurt, such as Cream Line Yogurt (Plain or Vanilla)

1 cup apple juice

½ cup frozen blueberries

½ cup frozen raspberries

½ banana

1 cup soy milk or milk of your choice

Prep time 5 minutes
Serves 2

1 Add all ingredients to a blender and purée until smooth. Keep refrigerated.

Nutrition Snapshot
Per serving: 309 calories, 7g fat, 3g saturated fat, 7g protein, 57g carbs, 5g fiber, 45g sugar, 112mg sodium

Beet and Goat Cheese Smoothie

Beets are underrated as a vegetable, which is a pity because they are very flavorful and a terrific source of iron. Although the combination of beet and goat cheese - in a smoothie no less - may seem a little daring, you will be amazed by the results. This recipe is just as good as it looks, with the beets contributing a velvety color and a sweet, earthy flavor that balances out the sharpness of goat cheese. I usually serve it with toasted bread wrapped in prosciutto, with Kalamata olives on the side.

1 (8-oz) pkg refrigerated **Steamed and Peeled Baby Beets**
½ (8-oz) pkg **Chevre Log** (goat cheese)
½ cup whole milk or milk of your choice
Pinch salt and pepper
1 tsp chopped fresh mint

Prep time 5 minutes
Serves 2

1 Add all ingredients except mint to a blender and purée until smooth. Sprinkle mint on top. Keep refrigerated.

Nutrition Snapshot

Per serving: 151 calories, 5g fat, 3g saturated fat, 11g protein, 15g carbs, 3g fiber, 12g sugar, 325mg sodium

California Gazpacho Smoothie

Gazpacho is a raw, chunky tomato and vegetable soup, a favorite appetizer in Spain and throughout the Mediterranean. Served chilled, it is very refreshing and especially popular during summer when tomatoes are plentiful and at the peak of flavor. This smoothie is ideal for those who prefer savory to sweet. I like to add avocado for a silky and soft texture.

3 medium tomatoes, sliced

1 avocado, peeled and cut in small pieces

½ English cucumber, peeled and sliced

¼ cup olive oil

¼ cup red wine vinegar

1 clove garlic, crushed

¼ tsp salt

Pinch black pepper

1-2 cups cold water

Prep time 10 minutes

Serves 2

1 Add all ingredients to a food processor. Pulse blend to a grainy purée, adding water as needed to yield a soupy, chunky consistency. The soup should not be completely smooth.

2 Taste and adjust seasoning with salt and pepper. Keep refrigerated.

Nutrition Snapshot
Per serving: 385 calories, 35g fat, 6g saturated fat, 3g protein, 18g carbs, 7g fiber, 6g sugar, 299mg sodium

Spinach and Pineapple Smoothie

It may seem that spinach is out of place in a smoothie, but a sweet smoothie is the perfect place to incorporate (i.e., disguise) healthy greens and other vegetables. Spinach brings high nutritional value and a wealth of antioxidants while adding a vibrant freshness to this smoothie. Sweet, intense pineapple and fresh orange juice shine, while simultaneously balancing the spinach.

2 cups baby spinach leaves
1 cup frozen pineapple chunks
1 cup freshly squeezed orange juice
1 cup almond milk or milk of your choice

Prep time 5 minutes
Serves 2

1   Add all ingredients to a blender
    and blend on high until smooth.

2   Transfer smoothie to a bottle or
    glass jar, and shake well before drinking.
    Keep refrigerated.

Nutrition Snapshot
Per serving: 112 calories, 2g fat, 0g saturated fat, 2g protein, 23g carbs, 3g fiber, 18g sugar, 39mg sodium

Zucchini and Chocolate Milkshake

Here is another example of introducing a vegetable to a sweet smoothie. Add a mild, low-calorie, and high-vitamin vegetable like zucchini to your favorite decadence – did I say chocolate? – without jeopardizing its taste. This smoothie is for chocolate aficionados who want to work on their diet while still indulging.

1 cup grated zucchini
1 ripe banana, peeled
2 Tbsp unsweetened cocoa powder
¼ cup **Almond Butter with Roasted Flaxseed** (crunchy & salted)
1 Tbsp sugar
2 cups almond milk
2 Tbsp honey

Prep time 10 minutes
Serves 2

1 Blend all ingredients in a blender until smooth, thick, and creamy.
Keep refrigerated.

Nutrition Snapshot
Per serving: 399 calories, 22g fat, 2g saturated fat, 11g protein, 49g carbs, 9g fiber, 32g sugar, 93mg sodium

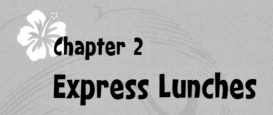

Chapter 2
Express Lunches

Sandwiches

Jambon-Beurre (French Ham and Butter Sandwich)

The jambon-beurre is to France what the hamburger is to the USA. The key to this iconic sandwich is to use the crispiest fresh bread, a good creamy butter, a tasty ham, and cornichons (tiny French pickles) – all of which are found at Trader Joe's. In this recipe I added cheese and tomato in order to pack a full meal in a baguette. Bon appétit!

½ baguette, preferably a **Par-baked French Baguette**, baked per instructions

1 tsp Dijon mustard

1 Tbsp unsalted butter, slightly softened

2 slices Gruyère cheese

3 slices **Rosemary Ham** or your favorite ham

½ tomato, sliced

2 cornichons

Prep time 10 minutes
Makes 2 sandwiches

Kids Favorites

1 Cut baguette open lengthwise. Spread mustard on one side and butter on the other side.

2 Cut each ham and cheese slice in half. Layer cheese, ham, and tomato over mustard. Slice pickles in half, and arrange on ham. Close sandwich, pressing well, and cut in half.

Nutrition Snapshot
Per sandwich: 426 calories, 16g fat, 9g saturated fat, 24g protein, 49g carbs, 2g fiber, 5g sugar, 972mg sodium

Pan Bagnat

This sandwich is essentially a salade Niçoise on a roll. Different filling combinations can be used, but tuna, olive oil, and tomato are ones that are always present. The full breadth of Mediterranean flavors is inside this sandwich, and biting into it will transport you right to Nice, France, where this sandwich was born. It is important to allow time for all the flavors to come together before eating. A picnic favorite!

½ **small red onion, thinly sliced**

½ **small white onion, thinly sliced**

2 **Tbsp olive oil, plus additional for drizzling**

1 **Tbsp red wine vinegar**

1 **(6-oz) can tuna packed in olive oil**

Juice of 1 lemon

Pinch salt and pepper

2 **ciabatta individual rolls**

6 **spinach leaves**

1 **large tomato, sliced**

2 **hard boiled eggs, sliced**

Nicoise or Black Olives (optional)

4 **anchovy filets, drained**

Prep time 15 minutes
Serves 2

1   In a bowl, mix red and white onion, oil, and vinegar.

2   In another bowl, mix tuna (including the oil), lemon juice, salt, and pepper.

3   Cut ciabatta rolls in half so that you have 4 round roll halves. Layer each bottom half with onions. Arrange spinach leaves and tomato slices on top.

4   Add tuna mixture, eggs, and olives on each sandwich. Criss-cross each sandwich with 2 anchovy fillets, drizzle generously with olive oil, and close top, pressing gently but firmly.

Nutrition Snapshot

Per serving: 581 calories, 21g fat, 4g saturated fat, 36g protein, 46g carbs, 4g fiber, 5g sugar, 749mg sodium

Crunchy Hummus Wrap

Made of fresh ingredients and store-bought hummus, this wrap is easy to assemble and transport. Crisp cucumber and carrot, sweet raisins, and fresh mint combine with hummus to create a symphony of flavors and textures in your mouth. It's a beautiful and satisfying wrap for vegetarians and vegans!

1 ½ cups hummus

2 Clay Oven Baked Whole Wheat Lavash Breads

1 ½ cups grated carrot

1 small cucumber, thinly sliced

⅓ cup golden raisins

6 fresh mint leaves, chopped

Prep time 15 minutes

Serves 4

    * Use brown rice tortillas

1 Spread hummus on each piece of lavash, leaving a 1-inch border around edges. Evenly layer carrots, cucumber, and raisins on each bread. Sprinkle with mint.

2 Fold sides of each bread toward center, and then tightly roll to enclose filling. Slice each roll in half.

Nutrition Snapshot

Per serving: 423 calories, 14g fat, 0g saturated fat, 11g protein, 61g carbs, 9g fiber, 14g sugar, 616mg sodium

Second to Naan Sandwich

Naan is an Indian oven-baked flatbread with a lovely, chewy quality that is wonderful in sandwiches. Biting into this colorful and sweet pork sandwich is a delightful invitation to an exotic place. Very simple to make, it combines international classics: Indian naan and chutney, Mexican carnitas, and Italian sun dried tomatoes. Peppery arugula rounds out the burst of flavors.

Prep time 15 minutes
Serves 4

4 fresh or frozen Naan
1 cup Mango Ginger Chutney
½ cup fresh arugula leaves
½ (24-oz) pkg Traditional Carnitas Pork Roast, cut lengthwise into thin strips
½ cup Sun-dried Tomatoes Preserved in Oil, drained

1 Toast naan using a toaster.

2 Spread chutney on each bread. Top with arugula.

3 Arrange pork strips on naan. Layer with sun-dried tomato pieces.

4 Close sandwiches and press well. Slice in half.

Nutrition Snapshot
Per serving: 473 calories, 11g fat, 3g saturated fat, 22g protein, 71g carbs, 4g fiber, 26g sugar, 800mg sodium

Smoked Salmon, Mint and Goat Cheese Bagel

This classic sandwich came to North America via Montreal and New York City through the immigration of many Russian and European Jews. A traditional smoked salmon Sunday brunch is such a pleasant and tasty experience. This recipe adds a twist by using mint and goat cheese instead of raw onion and cream cheese. The refreshing crunch of cucumber balances and complements the goat cheese and salmon. Serve as a main dish, as this is a filling sandwich.

2 bagels

5 oz **Chevre Log** (goat cheese)

1 clove garlic, minced, or 1 cube frozen **Crushed Garlic**, thawed

4 fresh mint leaves, chopped

½ **English cucumber**, peeled and thinly sliced

2 oz **Wild Smoked Salmon**

Prep time 15 minutes
Serves 2

1 Cut each bagel in half, so that you have 4 round bagel halves.

2 In a medium bowl, mix goat cheese, garlic, and mint, blending well.

3 Spread cheese mixture on bagel bottoms. Layer with cucumber slices and salmon, covering with bagel tops. Press well.

Nutrition Snapshot
Per serving: 302 calories, 6g fat, 2g saturated fat, 19g protein, 44g carbs, 2g fiber, 1g sugar, 825mg sodium

Vegetarian Club Sandwich

Who says vegetarians can't join the club? Even non-vegetarians will love the light but satisfying combination of fresh tomato, mozzarella, cucumber, and hummus. Use Tofurky deli slices or your own favorite combination of vegetarian meats or bacon.

4 slices sandwich bread
1 Tbsp mayonnaise
1 Tbsp hummus
2 slices **Hickory Smoked Tofurky** deli slices
½ English cucumber, peeled and sliced
1 small tomato, thinly sliced
4 oz mozzarella cheese log, cut into ½-inch slices

Prep time 5 minutes
Serves 2

1 Spread mayonnaise on two slices of bread. Spread hummus on remaining two slices of bread.

2 Assemble two sandwiches by layering deli, cucumber, mozzarella, and tomato between bread slices.

3 Press sandwiches shut and secure with toothpicks. Cut in half.

Nutrition Snapshot
Per serving: 392 calories, 18g fat, 9g saturated fat, 18g protein, 32g carbs, 3g fiber, 5g sugar, 728mg sodium

Chapter 3
Gourmet On The Run

Soups

La Vichyssoise

Traditionally served chilled in summer, vichyssoise is a classic French soup. Surprisingly, it was invented in New York City, albeit by a French-born chef who based it on the potato and leek soup made by his mother and grandmother. Thick and creamy, the soup takes full advantage of the subtle, sweet flavor of leeks. Despite their high nutritional and culinary value, leeks are still vastly underrated in America, where not many people seem to know how to prepare them. Luckily, Trader Joe's is now selling them trimmed and ready to use.

2 (6-oz) pkgs refrigerated **Trimmed Leeks**, chopped

½ white onion, chopped, or ½ cup refrigerated **Diced Onion**

1 Tbsp olive oil

1 Tbsp unsalted butter

3 small potatoes (approx. 10 oz), thinly sliced

5 cups chicken or vegetable broth

¼ cup heavy cream

3 chive leaves for garnish

Salt and pepper to taste

Prep time 10 minutes
Hands-off cooking time
30 minutes
Serves 6

* Choose
gluten-free broth

1 In a soup pot over medium heat, gently sauté leeks and onion in olive oil and butter for 5 minutes or until soft. Add potatoes and broth.

2 Bring to a boil on high heat for 5 minutes, and then reduce heat to low and simmer gently for 20 minutes until all vegetables are tender. If using low-sodium broth, taste soup and season with salt and pepper.

3 Purée in blender or food processor until smooth. Cool, then refrigerate until chilled. Gently stir in cream and chives before serving.

Safety Tip

In order to be safe, it is recommended that you do not fill the blender jar more than half full with hot soup. Cover the lid with a dry towel, and hold it down with your hand while puréeing to avoid the steam popping the lid open. Depending on how powerful your blender is, you may need to use some force to keep the lid on.

Nutrition Snapshot

Per serving: 228 calories, 11g fat, 5g saturated fat, 4g protein, 29g carbs, 4g fiber, 6g sugar, 597mg sodium

Chilled Cucumber Soup

Most cucumber soup recipes use raw cucumber mixed with heavy cream or yogurt. My mother's recipe calls for cooking the cucumbers in broth, then blending the soup before chilling. Cooking the cucumber makes the soup easier to digest and gives a better flavor than using raw cucumber. The creaminess of The Laughing Cow cheese imparts a smooth, velvety texture. Lovely!

1 tsp butter

1 tsp olive oil

½ white onion, peeled and chopped

1 English cucumber, peeled and chopped

2 cups chicken or vegetable broth

2 wedges **The Laughing Cow** spreadable cheese (light or original)

Salt and pepper to taste

Prep time 10 minutes
Hands-off cooking time
25 minutes
Serves 2

 * Choose
gluten-free broth

1   Add butter and oil to a soup pot over medium heat. Add onion; cook and stir for 5-8 minutes until onion is soft and transparent.

2   Add cucumber and cook 5 more minutes.

3   Pour in broth and bring to a boil on high heat for 5 minutes. Reduce heat and simmer for 10 minutes.

4   Add cheese and cook for 3 minutes. If using low-sodium broth, taste soup and season with salt and pepper.

5   Purée in blender or food processor until smooth. Cool, then refrigerate until chilled.

Note
See Safety Tip on p. 52

Nutrition Snapshot
*Per serving: 103 calories, 7g fat,
3g saturated fat, 4g protein, 6g carbs,
0g fiber, 3g sugar, 831mg sodium*

Carrot and Coconut Soup

This is an exquisite soup for the palate and the eyes. The gorgeous orange comes from the carrots and Thai yellow curry sauce, another splendid product sold at Trader Joe's. Coconut milk adds an exotic touch.

3 Tbsp olive oil, divided

1 sweet onion (such as a Vidalia or Maui onion), peeled and diced

1 clove garlic, minced, or 1 cube frozen **Crushed Garlic**

5 carrots, peeled and sliced

2 Tbsp **Thai Yellow Curry Sauce**

4 cups vegetable broth, chicken broth, or water

½ (13.5-oz) can coconut milk

Salt and pepper to taste

Prep time 10 minutes
Hands-off cooking time 30 minutes
Serves 4

* Choose gluten-free broth

1   Add 2 Tbsp oil to a soup pot over medium heat. Add onion; cook and stir for 5-8 minutes until onion is soft and transparent. Add garlic and cook for 1 minute more.

2   Remove onion and garlic from pot. Set aside.

3   Using the same soup pot over medium-high heat, cook and stir carrots in remaining oil for 10 minutes.

4   Add onion mixture, curry, and broth. Bring to a boil over high heat for 5 minutes, then cover and simmer for 20 minutes until vegetables are soft. Add coconut milk. If using low-sodium broth, add salt and pepper as needed.

5   Purée in blender or food processor until smooth. Pour hot into a Thermos jar, or refrigerate and reheat before eating.

Note
See Safety Tip on p. 52

Nutrition Snapshot
Per serving: 194 calories, 14g fat, 4g saturated fat, 3g protein, 16g carbs, 3g fiber, 6g sugar, 726mg sodium

Garlic, Garbanzo & Spinach Soup

This rustic soup is hearty and healthy, and, with the addition of the sausage, can be served as a full meal during winter dinners. Vegetarians can use soy chorizo instead of the sausage for an equally delicious result.

⅓ cup frozen **Organic Brown Rice** or leftover rice

2 cloves garlic, minced, or 2 cubes frozen **Crushed Garlic**

1 medium onion, chopped, or 1 cup refrigerated **Diced Onion**

2 Tbsp olive oil

5 cups vegetable broth, chicken broth, or water

2 small potatoes, peeled and cut in bite-size chunks

1 (15-oz) can garbanzo beans, rinsed and drained

1 cup frozen chopped spinach, thawed and drained

2 Bratwurst sausages, sliced in 1-inch pieces

Salt and pepper to taste

Prep time 10 minutes
Hands-off cooking time
35 minutes
Serves 6

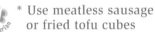 * Use meatless sausage
or fried tofu cubes

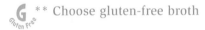 ** Choose gluten-free broth

1 Heat rice per package instructions. Set aside.

2 Add oil to a soup pot over medium heat. Add onion and garlic; cook and stir for 5-8 minutes until onion is soft and transparent.

3 Add broth, potatoes, beans, spinach, and sausage. Bring to a boil over high heat; reduce heat to low and simmer for 15 minutes.

4 Add rice; simmer for 5 minutes more. If using low-sodium broth, add salt and pepper as needed. Pour hot into a Thermos jar, or refrigerate and reheat before eating.

Nutrition Snapshot
Per serving: 210 calories, 9g fat, 2g saturated fat, 7g protein, 27g carbs, 5g fiber, 2g sugar, 757mg sodium

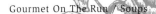

Chilled Peach Soup

I am very fond of chilled fruit soups. Of course, during the summer it is always better to use seasonal fruits, but when you do not have anything fresh on hand, substitute good quality canned or frozen fruits. Ripe peach and melon are household favorites for their subtle taste and juiciness. Maple-agave syrup and fresh mint add depth and complexity.

3 pieces jarred **Peach Halves in White Grape Juice**, drained
1 cup plain whole milk yogurt, preferably **Plain Cream Line Yogurt**
1 Tbsp **Organic Maple Agave Syrup Blend** or honey
Fresh mint leaves, chopped (optional)

Prep time 10 minutes
Serves 2

1   Add all ingredients except mint to a blender and purée until smooth. Stir in mint.

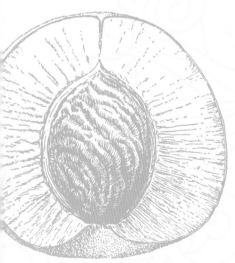

Nutrition Snapshot
Per serving: 231 calories, 5g fat, 3g saturated fat, 6g protein, 40g carbs, 2g fiber, 35g sugar, 78mg sodium

Chapter 3
Gourmet On The Run

Salads

Grapefruit Surprise

Using grapefruit rinds as cups adds a quaint touch to this unique salad. The tartness of the citrus mixed with delicate langostino tails and mayonnaise makes this dish refreshing and subtle in taste. Grapefruit, packed with vitamins B and C and antioxidants, boosts the immune system. For bolder flavor, add 1 tsp Dijon mustard. Prepare this dish ahead of time and leave it in the fridge until ready to serve.

1 pink grapefruit

1 cup frozen langostino tails, thawed and rinsed

⅓ cup reduced-fat mayonnaise

Salt and pepper to taste

8 arugula or baby spinach leaves

1 tsp fresh thyme

Prep time 10 minutes
Serves 2

1 Thoroughly wash grapefruit before cutting in half. Gently scoop out pulp with a teaspoon and dice segments, keeping juice. Place in a salad bowl. Discard white pith but reserve empty rinds to use as bowls.

2 In a salad bowl, mix langostinos, grapefruit pulp, juice (if any), and mayonnaise. Season with salt and pepper.

3 Fill each cup-shaped rind with langostino mixture. Top with arugula and thyme.

Note

In order to separate the skin from the flesh of the grapefruit, insert tip of knife into fruit where rind meets flesh. Hold blade up, then gently push it down until it nearly reaches bottom of shell. Run knife blade around perimeter of grapefruit and slowly turn fruit as you go to separate rind and flesh.

Nutrition Snapshot

Per serving: 217 calories, 9g fat, 0g saturated fat, 17g protein, 16g carbs, 2g fiber, 9g sugar, 462mg sodium

Lentil & Beet Salad

This scrumptious salad is essentially made of "super foods" – lentils, beets, and tomatoes. Green lentils are unique in flavor, a good source of iron, and an essential source of proteins for vegetarians. You can find green lentils in bulk in health stores and of course at Trader Joe's, where they are available steamed and ready to eat. Pour the vinaigrette on top of the lentils when they are still warm so that they will soak its flavor. This salad is best when made the day before.

½ (17.6-oz) pkg refrigerated **Steamed Lentils**

3 pearl tomatoes, cut in wedges

½ (8-oz) pkg refrigerated **Steamed and Peeled Baby Beets**, thinly sliced

3 oz goat cheese log, crumbled

Salt and pepper to taste

Chives and fresh thyme for garnish

Vinaigrette

2 Tbsp olive or vegetable oil

1 Tbsp red wine vinegar

1 tsp Dijon mustard

½ shallot, minced

Prep time 5 minutes
Serves 2

1 Place lentils in a medium bowl and heat in microwave for 3 minutes. Stir in tomato and beets.

2 Whisk vinaigrette ingredients.

3 Pour vinaigrette over lentil mixture, stir to combine, then sprinkle with goat cheese crumbles. Taste and adjust seasonings. Garnish with chives and thyme.

Nutrition Snapshot

Per serving: 396 calories, 21g fat, 7g saturated fat, 14g protein, 28g carbs, 9g fiber, 7g sugar, 477mg sodium

Peachy Chicken Salad

I am a big fan of the exotic combination of meat and fruits, especially in cold plates and salads. This salad is light and delectable, yet charged with nutrients and very simple to assemble. Other fresh or canned fruits like mandarin oranges can be used as a substitute for the peach. Prepare it the day before eating to allow the flavors to develop.

2 boneless skinless chicken breast halves or cooked **Just Chicken**

Pinch salt and pepper

3 Tbsp olive oil, divided

1 ½ Tbsp lemon juice

1 Tbsp white balsamic vinegar

3 pieces jarred **Peach Halves in White Grape Juice**, drained and cut in small chunks

⅔ cup raw walnuts (optional)

Handful **Baby Salad Mix**

Prep time 10 minutes
Hands-off cooking time 15 minutes
(0 minutes if using cooked chicken)
Serves 2

G
Gluten Free

·K·
Kids Favorites

1 If using cooked chicken, cut into strips and skip to next step.
   Season chicken breasts with salt and pepper. In a saucepan over medium heat,
   cook chicken breasts in 2 Tbsp olive oil for 5-8 minutes per side until cooked through.
   Place on a paper-towel-lined plate. Cool slightly. Cut into thin strips and set aside.

2 In a medium bowl, whisk 1 Tbsp oil, lemon juice, and vinegar.

3 In a large bowl, add peaches, chicken strips, nuts, and baby salad mix.
   Coat with vinaigrette and toss gently.

Nutrition Snapshot
*Per serving: 565 calories, 22g fat, 3g saturated fat,
30g protein, 60g carbs, 4g fiber, 47g sugar, 447mg sodium*

Tomato and Plum Salad with Wee Brie Sandwiches

How does one turn a simple tomato salad into the queen of all salads? Add the magical sweet and salty combination of plum and olives! Plums are loaded with vitamin C, vitamin A, iron, potassium, and dietary fiber. As for the olives, indulge in Trader Joe's Stuffed Queen Sevillano Olives from Spain. They are delicious, cholesterol-free, and an excellent source of monounsaturated fat, iron, vitamin E, copper, and dietary fiber. Serve salad with crunchy and creamy Brie mini-sandwiches.

7 **Pearl Tomatoes on Vine**, sliced

3 oz **Cherry Medley Tomatoes** or plain cherry tomatoes

1 plum, sliced

½ onion, thinly sliced

5 **Stuffed Queen Sevillano Olives**, chopped

Vinaigrette

1 Tbsp olive oil

1 tsp wine vinegar

2 tsp honey

Pinch each salt and pepper

Brie Mini-Sandwiches

2 oz. domestic Brie, sliced and cut to cracker size

8 **Organic Assorted Crackers**

Prep time 10 minutes
Serves 1

🍄 Vegetarian   **G** Gluten Free   * Use Savory Thins sesame crackers

1   In a large bowl, mix tomatoes, plum, onions, and olives.

2   In small bowl, whisk vinaigrette ingredients.
    Pour vinaigrette over tomato mixture and toss to coat.

3   To assemble mini-sandwiches, place each slice of Brie between 2 crackers.

Nutrition Snapshot

Per serving: 437 calories, 32g fat, 14g saturated fat, 12g protein, 38g carbs, 3g fiber, 20g sugar, 714mg sodium

Chapter 3
Gourmet On The Run

Sandwiches

Toasted English Muffins with Hummus

These little eat-it-on-the-spot sandwiches take full advantage of the delicious hummus dips carried by Trader Joe's. I decided to include them here after receiving an unexpected number of rave reviews on my Facebook page. Yes, they are delicious indeed. Thank you, friends!

3 English muffins

6 Tbsp hummus

1 medium tomato, sliced

1 medium ripe avocado, peeled and sliced

9 fresh basil leaves

Prep time 10 minutes
Makes 3 sandwiches

 Vegetarian Kids Favorites

1 Slice open English muffins and toast.

2 Spread 1 Tbsp hummus on each slice.
Make sandwiches with tomato, avocado, and basil.

Nutrition Snapshot
Per sandwich: 230 calories, 9g fat, 2g saturated fat, 7g protein, 35g carbs, 6g fiber, 2g sugar, 287mg sodium

Toasted Ciabatta with Red Pepper and Sardines

The benefits of omega-3 fatty acids in fish oil are well known nowadays. However, most people don't know that canned sardines are a great source of these healthy fats as well as calcium. Try sardines in sandwiches where you might typically use tuna. The combination of red bell pepper spread and sardines is wonderful and healthy.

½ **Par Baked Artisan Ciabatta roll, baked per bag instructions**
½ cup **Red Pepper Eggplant Garlic Spread**
2 **Skinless and Boneless Sardines in Olive Oil**, drained and halved
2 or 3 basil leaves

Prep time 10 minutes
Serves 1

1 Slice bread in half lengthwise and toast.

2 Smear red pepper spread on each slice.
Top one side with sardines and basil leaves. Close sandwich and press well.

Nutrition Snapshot
Per serving: 412 calories, 7g fat, 1g saturated fat, 18g protein, 64g carbs, 6g fiber, 6g sugar, 1,225mg sodium

Pita with Couscous, Raisins and Tofu

This highly portable pita sandwich showcases a medley of flavors and texture. Light, fluffy couscous preserves the sweetness of the raisins and grapes while emboldened by the exotic touch of Thai yellow curry sauce. The addition of tofu makes this sandwich very filling and satisfying. You may want to eat half with a soup or salad.

1 cup uncooked couscous (whole wheat or plain)

1 Tbsp olive oil

½ tofu block, pressed, drained and cut into 1-inch slices

½ cup red grapes, halved

1 Tbsp raisins

2 cloves garlic, minced, or 2 cubes frozen **Crushed Garlic**, thawed

1 Tbsp toasted pine nuts

¼ tsp salt

Pinch black pepper

2 Tbsp **Thai Yellow Curry Sauce**

2 pieces regular pita bread (halved)

Prep and cooking time
25 minutes
Serves 4

1 Cook couscous per package instructions. Set aside.

2 Heat oil in saucepan over medium-high. Add tofu; cook on both sides for 8-10 minutes total until golden. Drain on a paper towel and set aside.

3 In a medium bowl, mix couscous, tofu, grapes, raisins, garlic, pine nuts, salt, pepper, and curry sauce.

4 Stuff pita with couscous mixture.

Nutrition Snapshot
Per serving: 355 calories, 10g fat, 2g saturated fat, 14g protein, 54g carbs, 8g fiber, 8g sugar, 277mg sodium

Garlicky, Grilled Portabella Sandwich

Portabella, or portobello, mushrooms are robust and earthy, and even people who are not fond of mushrooms usually love this sandwich. Remember to remove the dark gills from the underside of the mushroom since the texture and color of the gills is not as appealing as the cap.

1 large portabella mushroom

2 Tbsp olive oil, divided

1 clove garlic, crushed, or 1 cube frozen **Crushed Garlic**

¼ red onion or 1 shallot, sliced

Pinch salt and pepper

6 oz tofu cut into 4 (½-inch) slices, pressed and drained

½ baguette, sliced lengthwise

1 Tbsp reduced-fat mayonnaise

1 Tbsp **Boursin Garlic & Fine Herbs** cheese

Handful baby spinach

Prep and cooking time
20 minutes
Serves 2

1 Scrape off dark gills on underside of mushroom. Remove and slice stem.

2 Heat 1 Tbsp oil in skillet over medium heat. When hot, add mushroom cap and stem, garlic, onion, salt, and pepper. Sauté cap for 3 minutes per side, while stirring other ingredients and brushing cap with olive oil if needed. Transfer to plate and set aside. Let cool, then slice mushroom cap into thick slices.

3 In the same skillet with remaining olive oil, sauté tofu slices on each side until browned. Remove tofu from skillet and drain on paper towel. Set aside.

4 Toast both bread slices.

5 Spread mayonnaise on one slice. Top with tofu, mushroom, onion, and spinach. Spread cheese on the other baguette slice. Close sandwich and press well.

Nutrition Snapshot

Per serving: 812 calories, 46g fat, 8g saturated fat, 34g protein, 72g carbs, 4g fiber, 3g sugar, 862mg sodium

Smoked Salmon in Herbed Pancakes

The idea of serving salmon with yogurt and pancakes is based on a traditional recipe with tiny Russian pancakes, called blinis, which are usually served with salmon and crème fraiche. Trader Joe's multigrain pancake mix makes, in my opinion, the best pancake from a box. Looking lovely and tasting amazingly good, this dish pairs wonderfully with a green salad.

For pancakes:

1 cup **Multigrain Pancake Mix**

½ cup milk

1 egg

1 Tbsp oil

⅓ cup finely chopped herbs (any combination of parsley, thyme, and basil)

For filling:

½ cup plain whole milk yogurt, such as **Plain Cream Line Yogurt**

1 tsp lemon juice

½ small onion, minced

Pinch salt and pepper

5 oz **Sliced Smoked Salmon**, shredded

⅓ cup **Micro Greens**

Prep and cooking time
25 minutes
Serves 4

1 Make pancake batter per box instructions. Stir in herbs. Set aside.

2 In another bowl, whisk yogurt, lemon juice, onion, salt, and pepper. Refrigerate until used.

3 Using herbed batter, cook 4 pancakes per instructions on box.

4 Lay pancakes on a plate. Top with salmon, add yogurt mix, and then top with micro greens. Roll pancake. Secure with a toothpick or kitchen twine.

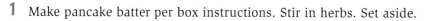

Nutrition Snapshot

Per serving: 267 calories, 9g fat, 2g saturated fat, 16g protein, 31g carbs, 3g fiber, 6g sugar, 662mg sodium

Originally from Japan, the bento box is compartmentalized to store an entire lunch in a single box. Vegetables, fish, meat, fruits, and cheese have their own place within the divided sections of a bento box, often with a theme and a pleasing aesthetic. The diversity of materials they are made of, the number of compartments they include, and the customization possibilities are such that it is possible to do something that is or feels different every day.

The first time I encountered a bento box was more than 10 years ago at the Tea Box Café located in the Takashimaya store in New York City. I was having lunch with a friend who was very familiar with the café menu. Having never before been to a Japanese tearoom, I ordered what she ordered. When the boxes arrived at our table, I was awestruck when the server removed the lid of the bento box and unveiled the contents. The bento box itself was absolutely gorgeous. The meal inside consisted of an elegant sampling of dishes thoughtfully arranged by the chef. I fell in love with the neat, organized presentation, and the taste of the food was delicate with a unique and inimitable *je ne sais quoi*. I thought, "what a great idea to serve food where everything has a special place!"

Taking advantage of Trader Joe's products from all over the world, I decided to assemble and design some international bento box menus using almost exclusively store-bought and ready-to-eat items. Most of the items shown in this chapter can be eaten at room temperature or cold, with only a few needing to be heated in the microwave. Assemble your meals in the morning or grab the items at Trader Joe's right before you eat. If you have a refrigerator or freezer available at work, buy the individual products and store them at work, assembling meals as needed.
This chapter provides examples to get your creative juices flowing, but you can assemble and create your own. Don't be intimidated! It is really fun, easy, and quick to do.

Chapter 4

International Bento Box

Indian Bento

Discover your inner vegetarian, and assemble this exotic and delicious meal composed of a curried lentil entrée served on basmati rice, a side dish of homemade samosa-style sweet pies, garlic naan (Indian flat bread), and yogurt with mangoes. **Āp kā khānā svādia ho!**

Box contents, clockwise from upper left:

Curried Lentils on Cumin Flavored Basmati Rice (frozen section), heated in microwave

Garlic Naan Bread (frozen section), toasted in a toaster

Plain Cream Line Yogurt and mango slices (fresh or frozen)

Samosa-Style Sweet Pies (see recipe p. 162)

Center: jarred **Mango and Ginger Chutney**

Italian Bento

Like you, I love all Italian food. This bento combines my love for Italian fare and distinctive Mediterranean flavors. The Gnocchi a la Sorrenta is just so delicious and perfect that I swear it could have been made by an Italian mama. Order an espresso café and some gelato and close your eyes … yes, you are in bella Italia! **Buon appetito!**

Box contents, clockwise from upper left:

Ciabatta bread, toasted, and prosciutto ham (deli section)

Gnocchi a la Sorrenta (frozen section), heated in microwave

Dried salami and prosciutto ham (deli section)

Almondina Original Biscuits (snacks & cookies)

Center: olive oil with olives

Japanese Bento

This bento is made using only the contents of Trader Joe's frozen Rice and Vegetable Bento Box. Take it with you when still frozen, and heat in only 3 minutes when ready to eat. I was surprised that it is tasty, light, and authentically Japanese. The nutritional content is agreeable as well: This bento is high in fiber, low in fat, and moderate in sodium. Above all, this assortment is 100% vegan. If/when this product is no longer available, simply use the list of contents as inspiration to create your own Japanese bento. **Douzo meshiagare !**

Box contents – all from one product, Rice and Vegetable Bento Box –
clockwise from upper left:

Brown rice with seaweed and sesame seed and eggplants with miso paste

Teriyaki flavored brown rice with vegetable and baked tofu with teriyaki sauce and edamame

Spicy long beans with curried flavored brown rice

Shitake mushrooms, soba salad with oyster mushroom, and pumpkin with shiso seasoning

Center: soy sauce

Mexican Bento

Living in Southern California near the Mexican border opened my eyes and palate to Mexican street food. Mini Chicken Tacos are a real time-saver and delicious served with guacamole, salsa, sour cream, or yogurt. They are simple to pack and eat: keep frozen, unwrap when you're ready to eat, cover with a paper towel, and heat for a couple of minutes. It's quick and easy enough for a workplace meal. The Spanish-style rice is made with frozen Organic Brown Rice mixed with salsa. **Buen provecho!**

Box contents, clockwise from upper left:

Organic Baby Spring Salad (refrigerated produce)

Mini Chicken Tacos (frozen section), room temperature or heated in microwave, and sour cream

Organic Brown Rice (frozen section), room temperature or heated in microwave, fresh salsa, and cherry tomatoes on skewers

Fresh orange slices

Center: Avocado's Number Guacamole (refrigerated)

American Bento

This bento would please and amuse any picky child. The mini hot dogs wrapped in puff pastry are too cute to resist, the Mac 'n' Cheese Bites are very savory and melt in your mouth, the vegetables with mayonnaise-yogurt are delicious, and the miniature brownie-cheesecake is an all-American dessert in one bite. **Enjoy your meal!**

Box contents, clockwise from upper left:

Mini Crispy Hot Dogs (see recipe p. 137)

Mac 'n' Cheese Bites (frozen section), room temperature or heated in microwave, or a serving of regular boxed or frozen mac 'n' cheese

Vegetable Salad (see filling from recipe p. 133)

Brownie-Cheesecake (bakery section)

Center: ketchup

French Bento

This menu is typically what Parisians eat during their lunch in a bistro: a jambon-beurre sandwich, Brie cheese, a lentil salad with a simple vinaigrette, and yogurt topped with a to-die-for caramel sauce for dessert. This bento is the only one with the decadence of two desserts! The Parisian macarons are a little treat people savor while drinking a strong black café after the meal. **Bon appétit!**

<u>*Box contents, clockwise from upper left:*</u>
Steamed Lentils (refrigerated produce), with vinaigrette (see recipe p. 67)
Jambon-Beurre Sandwich (see recipe p. 42) and Brie cheese
Parisian Macarons (frozen section), thawed
Plain Cream Line Yogurt and **Fleur de Sel Caramel Sauce**
Center: **Fleur de Sel Caramel Sauce**

Greek Bento

Greek cuisine is fresh with vibrant flavors: olive oil, lemon, feta cheese, oregano, and thyme. These ingredients give a burst of flavor to salads, yogurt, and, in the case of this bento, beans. Have you seen these jarred giant white beans in tomato sauce at Trader Joe's? They are really fantastic and tasty. For dessert, Greek yogurt topped with nuts, honey, and fresh fruit is just perfect! **Kalí óreksi!**

<u>*Box contents, clockwise from upper left:*</u>

Skanakopira (frozen section), room temperature or heated in microwave

Giant White Beans (Fasolia Gigantes), jarred

Homemade Greek tomato salad: medley cherry tomatoes, crumbled feta, olives, fresh thyme, and olive oil

Greek Yogurt with Nuts and Honey (see recipe p. 239)

Center: raw walnuts

Finger Foods

Lovely Olive Loaf

Called cake salé *in France, this savory cake started in one woman's booth at a Paris farmers market and exploded into a national phenomenon in France. This savory cake is a very versatile dish, easily adjusted to accommodate every taste. While olive and ham is the most popular combination, you can put a variety of ingredients – cooked chicken, sun dried tomato, chorizo, dates, or walnuts – in the batter with an equally superb outcome. Highly portable, it is ideally suited for brunch or any type of packed lunch.*

½ lb applewood cured ham steak

3 large eggs

1 cup all-purpose flour

1 tsp baking powder

½ cup warm low-fat (2%) milk

3 Tbsp olive oil

1 ½ cups grated Gruyere cheese or Swiss cheese

½ cup chopped green olives

¼ cup chopped black or Kalamata olives

½ tsp freshly ground black pepper

Prep time 15 minutes
Hands-off cooking time
45 minutes
 + 6 minutes for the ham)
Serves 8

* Omit ham. Substitute ¾ cup whole pistachio nutmeats.

1 Preheat oven to 350°F.

2 Cook ham steak per package instructions and cut into ½-inch cubes.

3 In a bowl, beat eggs, and then add flour and baking powder. Add milk and olive oil, a little at a time, whisking until smooth. Mix in ham, cheese, olives, and pepper.

4 Pour mixture into an oiled and floured standard loaf pan and bake for 45 minutes or until a knife inserted in center comes out clean.

5 Cool 10 minutes and cut into serving slices.

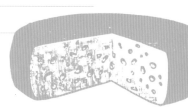

Nutrition Snapshot
Per serving: 301 calories, 16g fat, 5g saturated fat, 21g protein, 14g carbs, 1g fiber, 2g sugar, 826mg sodium

Crustless Tomato & Tuna Mini-Quiches

Everyone has heard of quiche. But tuna quiche? Bien sûr! You can make quiche with many different ingredients: goat cheese, leeks, salmon, zucchini … let your imagination run wild! This excellent recipe does not need a crust, thus it is preferable to use a muffin pan and create smaller quiches, which are easier to carry and do not need to be sliced.

2 Tbsp olive oil

1 small white onion, peeled and chopped, or ½ cup refrigerated **Diced Onions**

4 large eggs

1 cup low-fat (2%) milk

1 cup **Shredded 3 Cheese Blend**

½ tsp salt

¼ tsp black pepper

½ cup Roma tomatoes, chopped

1 (6 oz.) can Tuna in Water, drained and flaked

Prep time 10 minutes
Hands-off cooking time 25 minutes
Makes 12 mini-quiches

 * Omit tuna

1   Preheat oven to 375°F.

2   Oil and lightly flour a 12-cup standard muffin pan.

3   Add oil to skillet over medium heat. Add onion; cook and stir for 5-8 minutes until onion is soft and transparent. Stir in tomato. Remove from heat and set aside.

4   In a medium bowl, beat eggs, then stir in milk, shredded cheese, salt and pepper.

5   Portion onion-tomato mixture into muffin pan. Fill each muffin cup ½ full with egg mixture. Top with tuna. Sprinkle with salt and pepper.

6   Bake for 20-25 minutes, or until tops are lightly browned and a knife inserted near center comes out clean. Allow mini-quiches to cool before carefully removing from pan with a small knife or spatula.

Nutrition Snapshot
Per mini-quiche 69 calories, 4g fat, 1g saturated fat, 6g protein, 2g carbs, 0g fiber, 1g sugar, 189mg sodium

Ratatouille-Stuffed Bread

Inspired from popular paninis that are sold fresh and warm at Italian bakeries, this stuffed bread is an addictive delight. I opted for a larger portion that is sliced like bread, but you can easily adjust the proportions to your needs. Delizioso!

1 (1-lb) bag refrigerated **Plain Pizza Dough**

1 (13.4-oz) jar **Ratatouille** or 1 cup **Traditional Marinara** Sauce mixed with ½ cup **Eggplant Garlic Spread**

½ (12-oz) bag frozen **Fire Roasted Bell Peppers and Onions**

¼ tsp salt

¼ tsp freshly ground black pepper

7 oz **Mozzarella Cheese Log**, sliced

Prep time 10 minutes
(+ 20 minutes for dough to rise)
Hands-off cooking time 25-30 minutes
Serves 8

1 Preheat oven to 425°F.

2 Unwrap dough and leave at room temperature for 20 minutes.
Gently stretch dough to form a 15 x 8-inch shape. Place dough on a lightly oiled pan.

3 Spread ratatouille down center of dough lengthwise, avoiding the last inch at each end. Top with pepper-onion mix, salt, and pepper. Add cheese.

4 Carefully seal dough by bringing both long sides together in the middle like a long roll. Seal by pinching together the seam.

5 Bake for 25-30 minutes until crust is golden. Let sit for 10 minutes and slice into 1- or 2-inch pieces. Eat warm, cold, or at room temperature.

Nutrition Snapshot

Per serving: 256 calories, 9g fat, 4g saturated fat, 8g protein, 29g carbs, 3g fiber, 4g sugar, 838mg sodium

Broccoli, Cheese, and Crab Turnovers

Whatever you call these – chaussons, hand pies, turnovers, empanadas – they are essentially a piece of pastry folded over a filling. Hence they are very versatile and you can experiment with different fillings to suit your taste. The pink dipping sauce is whipped up in no time at all and is excellent with any fish or seafood plate.

1 cup refrigerated lump crabmeat

1 cup steamed and chopped broccoli florets

2 wedges **The Laughing Cow** spreadable cheese

Pinch salt and pepper

1 (10-oz) pkg frozen pie crust (2 sheets), thawed

1 large egg beaten with 1 tsp water for egg wash

Dip

2 Tbsp ketchup

2 Tbsp mayonnaise

Prep time 15 minutes
Hands-off cooking time 15 minutes
Makes 8 turnovers

  * Omit crab and use cooked and crumbled tofu instead.

1 Preheat oven to 375˚ F.

2 In a medium bowl, mix crabmeat, broccoli, cheese, salt, and pepper. Set aside.

3 On a lightly floured surface, unroll pie crusts and sprinkle each with a pinch of salt and pepper. Cut 16 round shapes (using a drinking glass) out of pie crust dough. Spoon ⅓-cup filling onto the centers of 8 rounds.

4 Using a pastry brush or your finger, moisten edges of the 8 filled rounds. Then top each with another round. Press edges of crust with the tip of a fork to seal. Gently prick holes into tops of each turnover to allow steam to escape.

5 Place turnovers on oiled or parchment-paper-lined baking sheet, and brush each with egg wash.

6 Bake for 13-15 minutes or until golden brown. Eat warm, cold or at room temperature. For the dip, mix ketchup and mayonnaise.

Nutrition Snapshot

Per turnover: 232 calories, 15g fat, 8g saturated fat, 8g protein, 15g carbs, 0g fiber, 2g sugar, 519mg sodium

Green Petite Bites

These muffin-like bites are a playful and scrumptious way to introduce kids and kid-like adults to iron-charged, antioxidant-rich spinach. Cute and appealing, they are very easy to make and literally melt in your mouth. You will be delighted to hear your kids asking for more, more, more!

2 Tbsp olive oil

½ cup refrigerated **Diced Onions**, or ½ medium white onion, chopped

1 cup frozen chopped spinach, thawed and drained

1 large egg, beaten

½ cup **Boursin Garlic & Fine Herbs** or **Rondelé Garlic and Herbs** (spreadable cheeses)

½ cup low-fat cottage cheese

Pinch salt and black pepper

Prep time 10 minutes
Hand-off cooking time 15-20 minutes
Makes 12 bites

1 Preheat oven to 375°F. Oil and lightly flour 12-cup mini muffin pan.

2 Heat oil in a skillet over medium heat. Add onion and cook for 3 minutes, stirring occasionally. Add spinach and cook for 5 more minutes. Set aside.

3 In a large bowl, whisk egg, and then stir in Boursin cheese and cottage cheese; mix well. Add spinach, onion mixture, salt, and pepper to bowl; mix well.

4 Portion batter into muffin cups to ¾ full.

5 Bake for 15-20 minutes until tops are lightly browned. Allow bites to cool before carefully removing with a small knife or spatula.

Nutrition Snapshot

Per bite: 75 calories, 7g fat, 3g saturated fat, 2g protein, 1g carbs, 0g fiber, 1g sugar, 135mg sodium

Green and Pink Egg Sushi

These colorful rolls may become a staple in your lunchbox. Healthy, adorable, and delicious, your kids will love them. The spinach-egg-mayonnaise combination is terrific and could be a full meal on its own. I used sandwich bread as a sushi roll to improve its portability and turn it into a finger food.

1 hard-boiled large egg, peeled and minced

1 Tbsp mayonnaise

1 tsp Dijon mustard

Pinch salt

Pinch black pepper (optional)

1 cup frozen chopped spinach, thawed and drained

1 Tbsp ketchup

4 sandwich bread slices, crust removed

Prep time 15 minutes
Serves 2

1 In a medium bowl, mix egg, mayonnaise, mustard, salt, and pepper (if using). Divide egg mixture between two small bowls.

2 Add spinach to one bowl and mix well; this is the green mixture. Add ketchup to the other bowl and mix well; this is the pink mixture.

3 Place one bread slice on a cutting board and roll with a rolling pin, flattening until thin. Repeat for each slice.

4 Spread spinach mixture on two flattened slices, and use a spoon to spread ketchup mixture on remaining two flattened slices. Do not use too much mixture on each slice. Roll each slice like a sushi roll, pressing firmly, and cut into bite-size rounds.

Nutrition Snapshot

*Per serving: 145 calories,
5g fat, 1g saturated fat, 6g protein,
17g carbs, 2g fiber, 4g sugar,
519mg sodium*

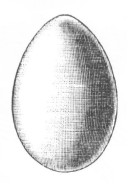

Mini Provençal Quiche

Just another quiche? Certainly not! This French classic is filled with subtle Mediterranean flavors and is as visually appealing as the Provençal landscape. Individual portions make it easier to capture big sun-drenched flavor in a small package. Ideally, make it the day before to allow the flavors to develop. This quiche is delicious cold or warm.

1 sheet frozen pie crust, thawed

3 Tbsp frozen **Fire Roasted Bell Pepper and Onion**

1 Tbsp chopped **Pitted Kalamata Olives**

2 Tbsp crumbled feta

1 Tbsp finely chopped fresh basil

2 jumbo eggs

¼ cup heavy cream

3 Tbsp low-fat (2%) milk

½ tsp black pepper

Prep time 10 minutes
Hands-off cooking time 20-30 minutes
Makes 4 mini quiches

1   Preheat oven to 375°F.

2   Divide crust into 4 equal parts. Using a rolling pin, roll each a 6-inch circle. Press pie crust inside 4 (4-inch) removable-bottom tart pans. Place in fridge until ready to fill.

3   In a large bowl, mix pepper-onion mixture, olives, feta and basil. Portion this mixture into crusts.

4   Beat eggs; mix in cream, milk, and pepper. Pour mixture into each crust, filling to ¼ inch below top edge.

5   Bake for 20-30 minutes or until puffed in center and golden brown on top.

Nutrition Snapshot

Per mini-quiche: 286 calories, 21g fat, 7g saturated fat, 10g protein, 22g carbs, 1g fiber, 1g sugar, 350mg sodium

Ham & Red Pepper and Cheese & Walnut Mini-Sandwiches

These mini-sandwiches are excellent for snacks or served as an hors d'oeuvre. The hearty combination of cheese and raw walnuts is unique in flavor and very popular with kids. The ham and red pepper combination is more intense and perfect for grown-up palates.

8 slices of white sandwich bread

2 Tbsp jarred **Red Pepper Spread with Eggplant and Garlic**

4 slices of **Rosemary Ham** or your favorite ham

2 wedges **The Laughing Cow** spreadable cheese or goat cheese

⅓ cup halved raw walnuts

Prep time 10 minutes

Makes 8 mini-sandwiches

1 Cut crust off bread.

2 Spread red pepper mixture on 4 slices of bread to make 2 sandwiches.
Place 2 folded ham slices on one slice, top with another slice of bread.
Repeat for the second sandwich. Press well and cut each sandwich in half.

3 Spread cheese on 4 slices of bread to make 2 sandwiches.
Place a full layer of walnuts on one slice, and then top with another slice of bread.
Repeat for the second sandwich. Press well and cut each sandwich in half,
using toothpicks to hold sandwiches together, if necessary.

Nutrition Snapshot
Per mini-sandwich: 130 calories, 5g fat,
1g saturated fat, 6g protein,
15g carbs, 1g fiber, 3g sugar, 353mg sodium

Zu-Corny Biscuits

*These zucchini and corn biscuits are easy to make, nicely accompanying soup or salad,
They are a delicious treat at brunch and great for a party when cut into finger food size,
Like many savory cakes or loaves, these biscuits are fitting as travel food as they can be
easily transported and eaten at room temperature.*

**2 cups self-raising flour (or 2 cups all purpose flour,
plus 2 tsp baking powder), sifted**

½ tsp salt

½ tsp black pepper

1 cup low-fat (2%) milk

1 egg, beaten

⅓ cup olive oil

½ cup grated Swiss or Gruyère cheese

1 small zucchini, grated coarsely

1 cup frozen **Roasted Corn** or regular corn kernels, thawed

½ cup refrigerated **Diced Onions**, or ½ medium-size onion, chopped

Prep time 15 minutes
Hands-off cooking time
20 minutes
Makes 12 biscuits

1 Preheat oven to 375°F.

2 Line a standard 12-cup standard muffin pan with paper baking cups,
   or lightly spray with oil.

3 In a medium bowl, mix flour, salt, and pepper. In another bowl mix milk, egg, oil,
   cheese, zucchini, corn, and onion. Gently stir wet mixture into flour mixture.
   Don't over-mix; mixture should be a little lumpy.

4 Portion mixture into paper baking cups. Bake for 20 minutes until lightly golden
   and a knife inserted near center comes out clean.

Nutrition Snapshot
*Per biscuit: 175 calories,
8g fat, 2g saturated fat, 5g protein,
20g carbs, 0g fiber, 2g sugar,
374mg sodium*

Italian Palmiers

Original palmiers, or elephant ears, are buttery, sweet cookies that are commonly sold at French bakeries. Looking for creative ways to increase the appeal of savory foods, I used Trader Joe's versatile puff pastry as a wrap that I shaped as palmiers. The trick here is to work quickly with a chilled pastry, which is more compact and easier to slice before baking.

1 sheet frozen puff pastry, thawed

1 cup jarred **Eggplant Garlic Spread**

5 slices prosciutto

5 fresh basil leaves

⅛ tsp salt

½ tsp black pepper

Prep time 10 minutes + 15 minutes chilling
Hands-off cooking time 20 minutes
Makes 24 palmiers

 *Omit prosciutto

1 Preheat oven to 400°F.

2 Place puff pastry on a lightly floured board. With a rolling pin, roll dough until it forms a 12-inch square.

3 Using a butter knife, spread eggplant garlic spread evenly on puff pastry. Top with ham, basil, salt, and pepper. Tightly roll both sides of square towards the center so that they meet in the middle. Brush water on seam in order to seal it. Place in fridge for 15 minutes.

4 When cold, slice dough into ½ inch slices with a sharp knife and place flat on oiled or parchment-paper-lined baking sheet.

5 Bake for 15 minutes. Turn each pastry slice over and bake an additional 5 minutes.

Nutrition Snapshot
Per palmier: 66 calories, 4g fat, 2g saturated fat, 1g protein, 6g carbs, 0g fiber, 2g sugar, 229mg sodium

Provençal-style Tomato and Mozzarella Loaf

This savory cake recipe is inspired by sun-kissed Provençe and the tomato-basil combination so prevalent there. Cheese adds a sharp taste to the medley of flavors while making the loaf softer and thicker. When well wrapped, this loaf keeps for 2-3 days at room temperature. If the slices become a little stale, toast them and use as bread for your next sandwich!

1 cup canned diced tomatoes, drained

4 Tbsp olive oil, divided

½ tsp salt

½ tsp freshly ground black pepper

7 oz whole mozzarella cheese, cut in ½-inch cubes

4 oz grated Gruyère cheese or Swiss cheese

8-10 fresh basil leaves, chopped

3 large eggs

1 cup all-purpose flour

1 tsp baking powder

½ cup warm whole milk

Prep time 15 minutes
Hands-off cooking time 45 minutes
Serves 8

1 Preheat oven to 350°F.

2 Mix tomatoes gently in a bowl with 1 Tbsp oil, salt, and pepper. Stir in cheeses and basil. Set aside.

3 In a separate bowl, beat eggs, and then add flour and baking powder. Add milk and remaining oil a little at a time, mixing until smooth. Add tomato mixture and mix well.

4 Pour mixture into an oiled and floured standard loaf pan. Bake for 45 minutes or until a knife inserted near center comes out clean.

5 Cool 10 minutes and cut into slices.

Nutrition Snapshot
Per serving: 285 calories, 19g fat, 8g saturated fat, 14g protein, 14g carbs, 1g fiber, 2g sugar, 485mg sodium

Pancetta and Ham Quiche Lorraine

Rightfully considered the mother of all quiches, the Lorraine is a quiche that most mothers in France bake weekly and serve with salad on the side. Every family has its own well-guarded recipe. This version takes all the basics of quiche Lorraine but uses bacon instead of lardons, which are similar in taste. I could not help but add another twist by using the delicious Italian pancetta cubes and rosemary ham from Trader Joe's. Encore!

2 Tbsp **Pancetta Cubetti** (pancetta mini-cubes)

1 Tbsp olive oil

1 sheet frozen pie crust, thawed

2 slices **Rosemary Ham**, shredded

2 eggs

½ cup low-fat (2%) milk

¼ cup heavy cream

5 oz **Cheddar Gruyère cheese** or regular cheddar, grated

Pinch black pepper

Prep time 15 minutes
Hands-off cooking time 30 minutes
Makes 4 mini-quiches

1 Preheat oven to 375°F.

2 Cook and stir pancetta in oil for 5 minutes (if using non-stick pan, oil is not necessary). Drain on a paper towel. Set aside.

3 Divide pie crust dough in 4 parts and roll each into a 6-inch circle, using a rolling pin. Line 4 (4-inch) tart molds with crusts.

4 Arrange pancetta and ham on bottom of each quiche crust. Beat eggs, and stir in milk, cream, cheese, and pepper. Portion mixture into crusts.

5 Bake for 20-30 minutes until top is golden brown and a knife inserted near center comes out clean.

Variation

Alternatively, you may make one large quiche. Use a 9-inch pie pan and single pie crust. Prepare filling as above but bake for 40 minutes or until a knife inserted near center comes out clean.

Nutrition Snapshot

Per mini-quiche: 467 calories, 36g fat, 15g saturated fat, 18g protein, 19g carbs, 0g fiber, 3g sugar, 637mg sodium

Pear and Brie Turnovers

These simple turnovers are a delicious savory-sweet dessert or snack. Creamy Brie nicely balances sweet pears. For bolder flavor, use goat or feta cheese. Brush the turnovers with a bit of egg wash right before baking to make the crust nice and golden.

1 sheet frozen puff pastry, thawed

1 egg beaten with 1 tsp water for egg wash

1 (8-oz) wedge double cream Brie

3 pieces jarred **Pears Halves in White Grape Juice**, drained and thinly sliced

Pinch salt and pepper

Prep time 10 minutes
Hands-off cooking time 15 minutes
Makes 9 turnovers

1 Preheat oven to 400°F.

2 Cut puff pastry sheet into 9 (3x3-inch) squares, like a tic-tac-toe grid.

3 Brush edges of each square with egg wash. Remove rind from Brie and cut cheese into 9 slices. Place 1 piece of Brie and 2-3 slices of pear at center of each square. Sprinkle with salt and pepper.

4 Fold each pastry diagonally to make triangles, and seal edges using a fork.

5 Place turnovers on oiled or parchment-paper-lined baking sheet, and brush turnovers with egg wash.

6 Bake for 10-15 minutes or until golden.

Nutrition Snapshot
Per turnover: 233 calories, 16g fat, 9g saturated fat, 7g protein, 15g carbs, 1g fiber, 5g sugar, 341mg sodium

Sweet-Savory Sticky Chicken

This sweet and flavorful chicken recipe tastes great hot or cold. The sauce used to cook the chicken is delightful and can be used with any meat or poultry. The oven-roasted and glazed drumsticks are a classic and a big hit with kids and finger food enthusiasts.

10-12 chicken drumsticks
½ tsp salt
½ tsp black pepper
½ cup balsamic vinegar
½ cup liquid honey
½ cup brown sugar
¼ cup soy sauce
5 garlic cloves, halved
1 Tbsp ketchup

Prep time 10 minutes
Hands-off cooking time 30-45 minutes
Serves 8

  * Omit soy sauce or substitute with tamari.

1 Preheat oven to 425°F.

2 Place drumsticks in 8x12-inch or 9x13-inch baking dish, optionally lined with foil for easy clean up. Season drumsticks with salt and pepper.

3 Mix vinegar, honey, brown sugar, soy sauce, garlic, and ketchup. Pour this mixture over drumsticks. Be sure to coat each piece well.

4 Bake for 30-45 minutes until chicken skin is caramelized juices run clear.

Nutrition Snapshot
Per serving: 267 calories, 7g fat, 2g saturated fat, 17g protein, 35g carbs, 0g fiber, 34g sugar, 875mg sodium

Ham and Cheese Croissants

These ham and cheese crescent roll-ups are an adaptation of a simple and popular French dish, widely used to recycle unsold or stale croissants. I entirely omitted the traditional béchamel sauce to make it lighter. If desired, add cream cheese inside the roll-ups for a nice velvety texture.

1 (8-oz) pkg refrigerated **Crescent Rolls**
4 slices **Rosemary Ham** or your favorite ham
4 slices Swiss cheese

Prep time 5 minutes
Hands-off cooking time 15 minutes
Makes 8 croissants

 *Omit ham

1   Preheat oven to 375°F.

2   Gently separate crescent dough into 8 triangles.

3   Using crescent triangles as a pattern, cut ham and cheese into similar triangular shape.

4   Place a piece of ham on crescent dough and top with a slice of cheese. Roll each croissant starting from widest edge to tip of triangle. Place on oiled or parchment-paper-lined baking sheet.

5   Bake 15 minutes until golden brown. Eat warm, cold, or at room temperature.

Nutrition Snapshot
Per croissant: 168 calories, 10g fat, 5g saturated fat, 9g protein, 13g carbs, 0g fiber, 4g sugar, 355mg sodium

My mother taught me how to use leftovers – transforming, assembling, and combining them to create a completely new dish. For *goûter* (French children's snacktime, also called *quatre-heure* – "the four o'clock"), she would use stale bread for bread pudding or *pain perdu* (French toast), and she would use leftover rice in delicious rice pudding.

My mother regularly made *pot au feu*, a vegetable and meat stew, from which she could serve three other meals based on the leftovers. She combined the broth with couscous and Gruyère to make a tasty soup; she used the vegetables in an amazing mashed potato-carrot-Gruyère dish; and she re-purposed the meat for melt-in-your-mouth meatballs.

Most refrigerators are full of leftovers: half a roast chicken, a bit of stale bread, a partly used can of beans, a bowl of mashed potatoes, and a few florets of steamed broccoli – all patiently waiting for a second chance. Another strategy is to create leftovers purposely by cooking extra batches of staple ingredients like beans, rice, or pasta. A simple pot of beans cooked once at the beginning of the week can be used again and again in various soups, salads, and wraps throughout the week. Using leftovers is not only efficient but very economical.

I recommend that you keep a pantry well stocked with different types of rice, pasta, beans, sauces, salsas, and spreads. Mixing and matching staple ingredients, leftovers, pantry helpers, and fresh ingredients will make wonderful and easy meals feel right at hand.

Chapter 6

Re-purposing
Leftovers

Chapter 6
Re-purposing Leftovers

Meats and Seafood

Savory Chicken Patties

1 cup finely chopped rotisserie or homemade roasted chicken

½ cup jarred **Eggplant Garlic Spread**

1 cup panko or breadcrumbs

⅓ cup grated Gruyère cheese

1 egg, beaten

2 Tbsp chopped fresh parsley

½ tsp salt

¼ tsp black pepper

2 Tbsp canola oil

Prep and cooking time
25 minutes
Makes 5 patties

  * Use almond meal instead of panko or breadcumbs

1 In a bowl, mix chicken with eggplant spread, panko, and cheese. Stir in egg, parsley, salt, and pepper; mix well.

2 Shape mixture into 5 patties, round and flat.

3 Heat oil in a skillet over medium-high heat. Cook patties for 3-4 minutes per side, until both sides are golden and crisp. Drain on paper towel. Pair with buns, if desired.

Nutrition Snapshot

Per patty: 240 calories, 14g fat, 3g saturated fat, 12g protein, 14g carbs, 0g fiber, 3g sugar, 663mg sodium

Honey Lemon Chicken Sandwich

1 cup chopped rotisserie or homemade roasted chicken

6 dried apricots

6 prunes

Zest of 1 organic lemon

1 tsp olive oil

2 Tbsp honey

1 tsp lemon juice

Salt and pepper to taste

2 slices sandwich bread

Prep time 5 minutes
Serves 2

  * Use brown rice bread

Kids Favorites   Gluten Free

1   Finely chop apricots and prunes.

2   In a bowl, mix chicken, apricots, prunes, lemon zest, oil, honey, juice, salt, and pepper.

3   Spread chicken salad between layers of bread.

Nutrition Snapshot

Per serving: 423 calories, 12g fat, 3g saturated fat, 22g protein, 61g carbs, 5g fiber, 40g sugar, 443mg sodium

Crunchy Baked Chicken Fingers

4 cooked boneless chicken breasts, cut into ½-inch strips

1 cup all-purpose flour

2 eggs, beaten

2 cups corn flakes, crushed

Pinch salt and pepper

1 Tbsp olive oil

Prep time 5 minutes

Hands-off cooking time 15 minutes

Serves 6

1 Preheat oven to 375°F.

2 Place flour, egg, and corn flakes into three separate bowls.

3 Dip each chicken strip in flour, then in egg, and finally in corn flakes, coating each strip completely. Season with salt and pepper.

4 Place strips on a non-stick baking sheet and drizzle with oil. Bake for 15 minutes or until golden.

Note

Kids can have fun crushing corn flakes with their hands and can help coat chicken strips.

Nutrition Snapshot

Per serving: 339 calories, 8g fat, 2g saturated fat, 40g protein, 24g carbs, 1g fiber, 1g sugar, 564mg sodium

Chicken Sausage Kebabs

4 cooked **Chicken Breakfast Sausages**, cut into thirds

1 tomato cut into small wedges

6 oz **Cheddar & Gruyère Melange Cheese**, cut into 6 cubes

3-6 salad leaves

Prep time 5 minutes

Makes 3 kebabs

1 Thread sausage, tomato, cheese, and salad leaves on 3 bamboo sticks, alternating ingredients.

2 Serve with ketchup or your favorite dip.

Nutrition Snapshot

Per kebab: 285 calories, 22g fat, 11g saturated fat, 20g protein, 2g carbs, 1g fiber, 1g sugar, 553mg sodium

Creamy Chicken and Veggie Salad

1 cup cubed cooked chicken or turkey

1 cup frozen **Vegetable Mélange**, heated in microwave

1 clove garlic, minced, or 1 cube frozen **Crushed Garlic**, thawed

1 Tbsp mayonnaise

1 Tbsp plain whole milk yogurt, preferably **Plain Cream Line Yogurt**

1 Tbsp ketchup

Prep time 5 minutes

Serves 2

1 Whisk garlic, mayonnaise, yogurt and ketchup.

2 Stir in chicken and vegetables until evenly coated.

Nutrition Snapshot

Per serving: 221 calories, 10g fat, 2g saturated fat, 22g protein, 10g carbs, 2g fiber, 5g sugar, 440mg sodium

Helpful Tip

Chicken is so versatile that leftovers are always welcomed in my fridge. I regularly roast my own chicken, choosing organic, free-range chickens because they are healthier and more flavorful than conventional chickens. A roasted chicken is simple to make and can provide a multitude of meals, with nothing going to waste. Serve the full bird as a main meal with a side of vegetables, rice, or pasta. Cut, cube, or shred the leftovers to make patties, fill a pita, or toss into salad. Freeze leftover chicken, pre-cut into bite-size pieces so that it's easy add to soups or stews. Finally, use the carcass to make homemade chicken stock, an amazingly rich base for soups. With all these options, you may consider roasting two chickens instead of one – double the food, ready in about the same amount of time.

Spicy Roast Beef & Arugula Sandwich

4 very thin slices **Boneless Beef Tri Tip Roast**, cooked per package instructions

½ par-baked or regular baguette

2 Tbsp **Wasabi Mayonnaise**

1 Tbsp **Black Pepper Sauce**

Handful arugula

Prep time 10 minutes

Serves 2

1 Cut baguette in half lengthwise and toast.

2 Spread mayonnaise on both halves of bread. Layer sandwich with meat, black pepper sauce, and arugula, closing with bread top.

Nutrition Snapshot

Per serving: 428 calories, 17g fat, 2g saturated fat, 24g protein, 48g carbs, 2g fiber, 4g sugar, 885mg sodium

Ham & Vegetable Roll Ups

4 slices **Healthy Cooked Ham**, Black Forest ham, or your favorite cooked ham
1 cup frozen **Organic Foursome** vegetable mix, cooked per package instructions
2 Tbsp reduced-fat or regular mayonnaise
2 tsp Greek yogurt

Prep time 10 minutes
Serves 2

1 In a bowl, mix vegetables, mayonnaise, and yogurt.

2 Put one slice of ham on a flat surface. Evenly spread 2 Tbsp vegetable mixture in a thick layer over ham.

3 Roll ham tightly. Secure with toothpick, if needed.

4 Repeat for remaining ham slices.

Nutrition Snapshot
Per serving: 140 calories, 5g fat, 1g saturated fat, 12g protein, 12g carbs, 2g fiber, 3g sugar, 480mg sodium

California Pork Sandwich

6 oz refrigerated **Fully Cooked Seasoned Pork Roast**, thinly sliced

1 par-baked **Artisan Filone bread**, baked, or any crusty Italian bread

4 Tbsp jarred **Eggplant Garlic Spread**

2 oz **Organic Pea Shoots** or alfalfa sprouts

1 avocado, thinly sliced

1 large tomato, thinly sliced

4 Tbsp reduced-fat or regular mayonnaise

Prep time 10 minutes
Makes 4 sandwiches

1 Slice bread horizontally. Spread eggplant garlic spread on one side.
Top with pea shoots, avocado, tomato slices, and pork.
Spread mayonnaise on other half of bread and top the sandwich.

2 With a large knife, cut each sandwich in two, making 4 sandwiches.

Nutrition Snapshot

*Per sandwich: 446 calories, 11g fat, 2g saturated fat, 16g protein,
67g carbs, 5g fiber, 4g sugar, 895mg sodium*

Mini Crispy Hot Dogs

1 frozen sheet puff pastry, thawed

25 **Cocktail Pups**
(uncured beef mini hot dogs)

1 egg beaten with 1 tsp water
for egg wash

Prep time 10 minutes
Hands-off cooking time 15 minutes
Makes 25 mini hot dogs

1 Preheat oven to 375°F.

2 Use pastry sheet as-is (do not roll or
stretch) and cut with a sharp knife
into 25 (2 x 2-inch) squares.
Place each square on oiled or parchment-
paper-lined baking sheet.
Brush each square with egg wash.

3 Place a mini hot dog on each square and
fold pastry around sausage.
Do not wrap completely.
Repeat for each hot dog.

4 Bake for 10-15 minutes or
until puff pastry is golden.

5 Serve with mustard or ketchup.

Nutrition Snapshot
*Per mini hot dog: 74 calories, 5g fat,
3g saturated fat, 2g protein, 4g carbs,
0g fiber, 0g sugar, 122mg sodium*

Focaccia and Prosciutto Mini Sandwich

12 slices prosciutto
1 (15 oz) **Tomato and Olive Foccacia** bread
1 cup jarred **Red Pepper Tapenade**
18 mixed medley or plain cherry tomatoes, halved
1 cup whipped cream cheese

Prep time 10 minutes
Makes 6 mini sandwiches

1 Cut focaccia into 6 (4 x 3-inch) rectangles. Slice each rectangle in half lengthwise with a knife.

2 Spread tapenade on bottom slices of focaccia and cream cheese on top slices. Assemble sandwiches by topping each bottom slice with one prosciutto slice folded in half, 6 halved cherry tomatoes, and one more prosciutto slice folded in half. Top with focaccia and press down to secure sandwiches.

Nutrition Snapshot
Per mini sandwich: 385 calories, 21g fat, 11g saturated fat, 19g protein, 34g carbs, 1g fiber, 5g sugar, 1712mg sodium

Seaside Pasta Salad

2 cups cooked penne pasta

1 cup frozen langostino tails, thawed, rinsed, and drained

1 cup refrigerated canned crabmeat, drained

1 cup cooked asparagus, cut in small pieces

½ cup reduced-fat or regular mayonnaise

1 Tbsp olive oil

Salt and pepper to taste

1 tsp white balsamic vinegar

Prep time 10 minutes

Serves 4

1 In a large bowl, combine pasta, langostinos, crab, asparagus, mayonnaise, oil, salt, pepper, and vinegar.

2 Gently toss and adjust seasonings if needed.

Nutrition Snapshot

Per serving: 304 calories, 14g fat, 2g saturated fat, 15g protein, 31g carbs, 2g fiber, 6g sugar, 677mg sodium

Salmon and Asparagus Tartlets

4 oz refrigerated Wild Alaskan Salmon, cooked and flaked

1 frozen pie crust, thawed

2 tsp olive oil

½ small onion, diced or ½ cup refrigerated **Diced Onion**

3 oz cooked asparagus spears, cut in half

3 large eggs

½ cup cream cheese

2 oz shredded mozzarella cheese

Pinch salt

¼ tsp black pepper

Prep time 15 minutes
Hands-off cooking time 20 minutes
Makes 6 mini tarts

1 Preheat oven to 375°F.

2 Roll and slightly stretch pie crust. Cut 6 circles that are roughly 6 inches in diameter. Place crusts into 6 (4-inch) round tart pans. Trim and crimp edges of dough. Prick bottom and sides of crust with fork. Place in fridge.

3 Heat oil in a saucepan over medium heat. Add onion and asparagus and cook for 5-8 minutes until onion is soft and translucent.

4 In a bowl, mix salmon, eggs, cream cheese, mozzarella, salt, and pepper.

5 Fill bottoms of tart shells with onion-asparagus mixture. Portion salmon mixture into tarts, over onion and asparagus.

6 Bake for 15-20 minutes or until filling is set and golden. Let cool on rack.

Did you know?

Coldwater fish such as salmon and tuna, whether frozen, canned, or fresh, are a good source of omega-3 fatty acids, protein, and other nutrients. Did you know that they contain higher levels of vitamin C Per serving: than oranges and lemons? Because of their dietary value, nutritionists recommend that we eat fish at least twice a week, but most people don't meet this goal. Try to get into the habit of enjoying fresh fish once a week and making use of leftovers in other recipes throughout the week.

Nutrition Snapshot

Per mini tart: 275 calories, 20g fat, 7g saturated fat, 12g protein, 13g carbs, 1g fiber, 2g sugar, 395mg sodium

Tuna in Tomato

¼ cup canned tuna in olive oil, drained

8 pearl or small Roma tomatoes

⅓ cup cooked quinoa

Pinch salt and pepper

1 Tbsp olive oil

1 tsp lemon juice

Prep time 10 minutes
Makes 8 stuffed tomatoes

1 Cut tops off each tomato with a paring knife, reserving for step 3 (optional). Spoon out seeds and pulp.

2 In a bowl, mix tuna, quinoa, salt, pepper, oil, and lemon juice.

3 Fill each tomato with quinoa mixture. Cover with tomato top, if desired. Refrigerate until ready to eat.

Helpful Tip

Canned tuna, packed in olive oil or in water, is a great staple in any pantry as a valuable addition to salads, pasta, or sandwiches. Buy canned light tuna made with skipjacks, a smaller species that contains about one-third the mercury levels of the albacore used in other canned tuna.

Nutrition Snapshot

Per stuffed tomato: 150 calories, 9g fat, 1g saturated fat, 7g protein, 10g carbs, 2g fiber, 2g sugar, 147mg sodium

A Tale of Two Salmons

2 oz Alaskan wild salmon, cooked and flaked

2 oz Alaskan smoked salmon, shredded in ½-inch strips

1 cup uncooked fusilli or penne pasta

2 tsp olive oil

4 stuffed **Queen Sevillano Olives**, chopped

Salt to taste

¼ tsp black pepper

1 cup herb salad mix

Prep and cooking time 15 minutes

Serves 2

1 Bring a large pot of lightly salted water to a boil. Add pasta and cook for 11-13 minutes or until al dente. Drain and place in a salad bowl.

2 Pour oil on pasta while still warm, and add salmon, olives, salt, and pepper. Add salad and toss gently. Refrigerate.

Nutrition Snapshot

Per serving: 244 calories, 10g fat, 1g saturated fat, 17g protein, 23g carbs, 3g fiber, 1g sugar, 779mg sodium

Fancy Shrimp Sandwich

2 cups frozen langostino tails, thawed and rinsed
½ **Tomato and Olive Focaccia Bread**
Salt to taste
¼ tsp black pepper
2 Tbsp **Wasabi Mayonnaise**
1 Tbsp fresh dill

Prep time 15 minutes
Makes 6 sandwiches

1 With a sharp knife, cut focaccia into 6 (3 x 3-inch) squares.
Slice each square in half lengthwise as per a small sandwich.

2 In a bowl, mix langostinos, salt, pepper, and mayonnaise.

3 To assemble each sandwich, spread langostino mixture on one side of bread,
add dill, and top with top slice of bread.

Nutriton Snapshot

*Per sandwich: 137 calories, 6g fat, 1g saturated fat, 9g protein,
13g carbs, 0g fiber, 0g sugar, 293mg sodium*

Vietnamese Roll

1 cup refrigerated canned crabmeat, drained and flaked

4 cooked asparagus spears, cut in small pieces

½ par-baked baguette or regular baguette

1 peeled carrot

⅓ cup reduced-fat or regular mayonnaise

Salt and pepper to taste

1 tsp chopped fresh mint

1 tsp chopped fresh cilantro

Prep and cooking time 10 minutes
Serves 2

1 Steam asparagus, or cook in microwave per package instructions. Set aside.

2 Cut bread in half lengthwise, leaving one side attached.

3 Using a vegetable peeler, cut carrot into long, thin ribbons.

4 In a bowl, combine crab, asparagus, mayonnaise, salt, and pepper.

5 Fill bread with crab mixture. Top with carrot ribbons and fresh herbs.

Nutrition Snapshot
Per serving: 245 calories, 8g fat, 0g saturated fat, 17g protein, 25g carbs, 3g fiber, 6g sugar, 1054mg sodium

Chapter 6
Re-purposing Leftovers

Vegetables and Legumes

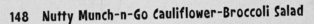

Nutty Munch-n-Go Cauliflower-Broccoli Salad

4 cups cooked broccoli and/or cauliflower florets
or 1 (16-oz) bag **Broccoli and Cauliflower Duet**, cooked

4 slices **Fully Cooked Uncured Bacon**

1 Tbsp olive oil

½ small onion, chopped

1 clove garlic, minced, or 1 cube frozen **Crushed Garlic**

¼ cup toasted pine nuts

Salt and pepper to taste

⅓ cup Manchego cheese or other sharp cheese, cut into thin ribbons

Dressing

½ cup plain whole milk yogurt, preferably **Plain Cream Line Yogurt**

1 tsp organic lemon zest

1 Tbsp olive oil

Salt and pepper to taste

Prep and cooking time 15 minutes
Serves 4

  * Substitute vegetarian bacon

1 Microwave bacon for 1 minute to reheat, then crumble when cool enough to touch.

2 Heat oil in a saucepan over medium heat. Add onion. Cook and stir onion for 5-8 minutes until soft and transparent. Add garlic and cook for 1 minute more. Set aside.

3 In a large bowl, combine broccoli, cauliflower, bacon, onion-garlic mixture, pine nuts, salt, and pepper.

4 In a small bowl, whisk dressing ingredients. Add dressing to salad and toss to coat. Top with cheese.

Nutrition Snapshot
Per serving: 230 calories, 17g fat, 6g saturated fat, 9g protein, 9g carbs, 4g fiber, 5g sugar, 249mg sodium

Asparagus and Spinach Frittata

12 cooked asparagus spears

2 cups frozen chopped spinach, cooked and drained

2 Tbsp olive oil

2 Italian sweet sausages with casing removed

1 clove garlic, minced, or 1 cube frozen **Crushed Garlic**

Pinch salt and pepper

5 large eggs, beaten

1 cup **Shredded 3 Cheese Blend**

Prep time 25 minutes

Hands-off cooking time 20 minutes

Serves 6

  * Substitute ½ pkg Soy Chorizo or other meatless sausage.

1 Preheat oven to 350°F.

2 Cut asparagus in 2-inch pieces.

3 Choose a cast iron skillet or other pan that can go into the oven.
Heat oil in pan over medium-high heat. Add sausages and cook for 8-10 minutes, breaking them into crumbles, until cooked through. Add asparagus, spinach, garlic, salt, and pepper. Cook and stir for 5 more minutes.

4 Pour eggs evenly over sausage mixture and cook for 6-8 minutes on low heat, without stirring or disturbing the pan, until eggs are mostly set.

5 Transfer pan to oven. Bake for 10-15 minutes or until fritatta is firm.
Sprinkle with cheese while still in oven. Turn oven off and let frittata sit in oven for 5 minutes more. Remove from oven, let cool, and cut into wedges.
Eat cold, warm, or at room temperature.

Nutrition Snapshot
Per serving: 234 calories, 17g fat, 7g saturated fat, 16g protein, 4g carbs, 1g fiber, 2g sugar, 398mg sodium

Broccoli Bacon Bisque

1 lb cooked broccoli, cut in small pieces

2 small potatoes, peeled and thinly sliced

1 clove garlic, minced, or 1 cube frozen **Crushed Garlic**

3 slices bacon, preferably Applewood uncured bacon

2 cups chicken or vegetable broth or water

2 cups low-fat milk

¼ cup heavy cream (optional)

Prep time 5 minutes
Cooking time 25 minutes
Serves 4

 * Use gluten-free broth

1 In a large pot over high heat, combine potato, garlic, bacon, and broth. Bring to a boil. Reduce heat and simmer 10 minutes.

2 Add broccoli to pot and return to a boil over high heat. Reduce heat and simmer, uncovered, about 5 minutes longer, until potatoes are tender when pierced. Add milk.

3 Purée soup with an immersion blender, or blend soup in batches with a blender.

4 Add heavy cream, if desired.

Helpful Tip

Leftover vegetables are a fantastic source of nutrients, color, and texture. Freeze small amounts of various leftover vegetables and use them to make a quick and healthy soup when you have collected enough.

Nutrition Snapshot

Per serving: 195 calories, 5g fat, 3g saturated fat, 11g protein, 28g carbs, 5g fiber, 10g sugar, 495mg sodium

French Green Bean Salad

1 cup frozen or fresh haricots verts (French green beans), cooked

3 slices bacon, preferably applewood uncured bacon, cooked and crumbled

2 tsp olive oil

1 tsp red wine vinegar

Pinch salt and pepper

2 oz goat cheese, crumbled

Prep time 5 minutes

Serves 2

  * Substitute vegetarian bacon.

1 In a large bowl, mix haricots verts, bacon, oil, vinegar, salt, and pepper.

2 Sprinkle with crumbled goat cheese.

Nutrition Snapshot

Per serving: 197 calories, 15g fat, 9g saturated fat, 11g protein, 4g carbs, 1g fiber, 2g sugar, 416mg sodium

Roasted Pepper and Carrot Quesadilla

4 carrots, peeled and cooked

¼ cup whipped cream cheese

⅓ cup frozen **Fire Roasted Bell Peppers and Onions**, thawed

¼ tsp salt

¼ tsp black pepper

Olive oil spray

2 flour tortillas

2 oz mozzarella, thinly sliced or shredded

Prep and cooking time 10 minutes
Serves 2

1 Mash carrots with a fork or in a food processor. Add cream cheese, pepper-onion mixture, salt, and pepper. Mix well.

2 Heat a large cast iron skillet over medium-high heat. Spray olive oil on bottom of the pan. Place one tortilla in the pan for 2 minutes, flipping it over every 10 seconds until both sides are very lightly golden.

3 Sprinkle cheese over tortilla, then dollop half the carrot mixture evenly over tortilla.

4 Reduce heat to low. When cheese is melting, use a spatula to fold tortilla in half. Cook 2-3 minutes until quesadilla is lightly browned and crisped on both sides. Remove from pan and cut into wedges. Repeat with the other tortilla.

5 Serve with guacamole or salsa.

Nutrition Snapshot
*Per serving: 394 calories, 16g fat,
10g saturated fat, 15g protein,
52g carbs, 10g fiber, 20g sugar, 913mg sodium*

Veggie Pancake with Pink Sauce

1 cup frozen **Vegetable Mélange**, cooked per package instructions

½ cup **Multigrain Pancake Mix**

1 egg

½ cup whole milk

2 Tbsp canola oil, divided

¼ tsp salt

¼ tsp black pepper

Dipping sauce

1 Tbsp ketchup

1 Tbsp mayonnaise

1 Tbsp plain yogurt

Salt and pepper to taste

Prep and cooking time 30 minutes
Serves 4

1　In a mixing bowl, whisk pancake mix, egg, milk, 1 Tbsp oil, salt, and pepper.
　Stir in vegetable mélange.

2　Heat 1 Tbsp oil in a large skillet over medium heat.
　Using a ladle, pour batter into pan, making one large, thick pan-size pancake.

3　Cook for 5-10 minutes – watch bubbles on top form and pop; when bubbles no
　longer pop, slides pancake onto a plate. Cover with another plate and flip.
　Slide pancake back into pan and reduce heat to low.
　Cook for another 5-7 minutes or until pancake is firm and cooked on both sides.

4　Let cool for 3 minutes. Cut in 8 wedges.

5　Whisk dipping sauce ingredients and serve with pancakes.

Nutrition Snapshot

Per serving: 168 calories, 12g fat, 2g saturated fat,
4g protein, 11g carbs, 1g fiber, 4g sugar, 338mg sodium

Carrot Flan

5 cooked carrots, peeled and chopped

2 cooked zucchini, peeled and chopped

1 cup whole milk

2 Tbsp butter

½ tsp salt

½ tsp black pepper

2 small eggs, beaten

1 Tbsp plus 1 tsp flour

Prep time 10 minutes
Hands-off cooking time
20 minutes
Makes 12 mini flans

1 Preheat oven to 375°F.

2 Lightly oil a 12-cup standard muffin pan or 12 ramekins.

3 In a saucepan, heat milk and butter over medium-low heat.

4 Place zucchini and carrot in a blender or food processor.
Add milk-butter mixture, salt, and pepper. Purée.
Add egg and flour to blender, and purée until smooth.

5 Portion mixture into muffin cups, filling almost to the top.

6 Add an inch of water to a large roasting pan. Set on an oven rack and then
place muffin pan inside roasting pan. Do not allow the water level to go over
the side of muffin pan or ramekin. Carefully push in rack and close oven door.

7 Bake for 15-20 minutes or until set. Eat warm, cold, or at room temperature.

Nutrition Snapshot

*Per mini-flan: 68 calories, 3g fat, 2g saturated fat, 2g protein,
7g carbs, 2g fiber, 4g sugar, 154mg sodium*

Maple Rustica Carrots with Almonds

1 (16-oz) bag frozen **Rustica Carrots**, cooked,
or 2 ½ cups leftover chopped and cooked carrots

¼ tsp salt

¼ tsp black pepper

1 Tbsp olive oil

1 Tbsp organic orange zest

¼ cup organic orange juice

1 tsp honey

1 Tbsp **Maple Agave Syrup Blend** or maple syrup

2 Tbsp sliced almonds

Prep time 10 minutes
Serves 2

Vegetarian   Gluten Free   Kids Favorites

1 Heat carrots in microwave for 3 minutes.

2 Mix warm carrots with salt, pepper, oil, zest, juice, honey, and syrup.
   Sprinkle with almonds.

Nutrition Snapshot
*Per serving: 228 calories, 10g fat, 1g saturated fat, 1g protein,
33g carbs, 6g fiber, 22g sugar, 441mg sodium*

Samosa-Style Sweet Pies

3 sweet potatoes, cooked and mashed
¼ tsp salt
¼ tsp black pepper
1 ½ Tbsp **Mango Ginger Chutney**
1 Tbsp creamy peanut butter
1 frozen pie crust, thawed
1 egg beaten with 1 tsp water for egg wash

Prep time 10 minutes
Hands-off cooking time
15-20 minutes
Makes 4 pies

1 Preheat oven to 375°F.

2 In a bowl, mix sweet potatoes, salt, pepper, chutney, and peanut butter. Set aside.

3 On a lightly floured surface, roll and stretch pie crust to a 12-inch diameter. With a 3-inch round cookie cutter or a drinking glass, cut 8 circles; these will make 4 pies.

4 Portion sweet potato mixture onto 4 crusts, mounding filling on center and leaving a ½-inch border.

5 Using a finger or a pastry brush, lightly brush water onto edges of filled crust. Top each with remaining crusts and press edges firmly to seal. Using a fork, crimp edges. Transfer pies to a baking sheet lined with parchment paper. Brush pies with egg wash.

6 Bake for 15-20 minutes until pies are golden.

Nutrition Snapshot

Per pie: 290 calories, 13g fat, 2g saturated fat, 5g protein, 36g carbs, 4g fiber, 8g sugar, 438mg sodium

Potato and Cauliflower Salad

3 small potatoes, peeled and cooked

1 head cauliflower, separated into florets

4 Tbsp olive oil, divided

Salt and pepper to taste

½ kielbasa sausage (optional)

¼ cup minced shallot or onion

1 clove garlic, minced, or 1 cube frozen **Crushed Garlic**

2-3 sprigs fresh thyme

1 cup plain whole milk yogurt, preferably **Plain Cream Line Yogurt**

½ Tbsp lemon juice

Prep and cooking time 30 minutes
Serves 4

1 In a skillet over medium-high heat, cook and stir cauliflower florets in 2 Tbsp
   olive oil for 5-8 minutes. Add 1 Tbsp water, simmer and stir. Cook until crisp-tender.
   Add salt and pepper. Transfer to large bowl and set aside.

2 In the same skillet, heat 1 Tbsp olive oil over medium heat. Add sausage, if desired,
   and cook for 7-10 minutes until brown and cooked through. Set aside and let cool.

3 Cut potatoes in bite-size pieces and place in bowl with cauliflower.

4 Cut sausage in bite-size pieces and add to the bowl. Add shallot, garlic, and thyme.
   Mix gently and add remaining oil.

5 In a small bowl, whisk yogurt and lemon juice. Pour this mixture over potato-
   cauliflower salad. Adjust seasoning if needed.

Nutrition Snapshot
*Per serving: 294 calories, 16g fat, 3g saturated fat, 7g protein,
32g carbs, 7g fiber, 8g sugar, 83mg sodium*

Spanish Potato Omelet

3 small potatoes, peeled, cooked, and thinly sliced

2 Tbsp olive oil

1 medium onion, very finely sliced

½ tsp salt, divided

½ tsp black pepper, divided

5 large eggs

¼ cup milk

Prep and cooking time
30 minutes

Serves 4

1 Heat oil in a skillet over medium heat. Add onion; cook and stir onion for 5-8 minutes until soft and transparent.

2 Add potatoes and half the salt and pepper. Reduce heat to low.

3 In a bowl, beat eggs with milk and remaining salt and pepper.

4 Pour egg mixture over onions and potatoes, making sure that all potatoes are covered. Without stirring, let egg set for about 10 minutes, then remove from heat.

5 Transfer omelet onto a plate. Cover with another plate and flip. Slide omelet back into pan over low heat. Cook for another 5-7 minutes or until omelet is firm.

6 Transfer to plate. Cut in wedges when cool. Serve warm, cold, or at room temperature.

Nutrition Snapshot

Per serving: 245 calories, 13g fat, 3g saturated fat, 10g protein, 23g carbs, 3g fiber, 3g sugar, 382mg sodium

French Potato Salad

9 small potatoes, boiled and peeled
2 Tbsp chopped herbs (any combination of fresh parsley, fresh thyme, or chives)
1 shallot, peeled and minced
3 small cornichons (small gherkin pickles), finely diced
Salt and pepper to taste

Dressing
2 tsp Dijon mustard
¼ cup red wine vinegar
Pinch salt and pepper
½ cup olive oil

Prep time 5 minutes
Serves 4

 Vegetarian Gluten Free

1 Cut potatoes into bite-size chunks. Place in large bowl.
Add herbs, shallots, cornichons, salt, and pepper.

2 To prepare dressing, combine mustard, vinegar, salt, and pepper in a small bowl.
Slowly pour in olive oil and whisk.

3 Pour dressing onto salad and toss gently. Serve warm, cold, or at room temperature.

Nutrition Snapshot
Per serving: 529 calories, 27g fat, 4g saturated fat, 7g protein,
62g carbs, 9g fiber, 5g sugar, 165mg sodium

Mini Potato-Cheese Patties

2 medium peeled potatoes, cooked and mashed,
or ⅔ cup leftover mashed potatoes

1 cup **Shredded 3 Cheese Blend**, divided

2 wedges **The Laughing Cow** spreadable cheese
(Original, Light or Garlic & Herb)

¼ tsp salt

Pinch black pepper (optional)

Prep time 5 minutes
Hands-off
cooking time 15 minutes
Makes 12 patties

1 Preheat oven to 375°F.

2 Butter or lightly oil a 12-cup mini muffin pan.

3 In a bowl, combine potatoes, ½ cup shredded cheese, spreadable cheese,
salt, and pepper (if using). Mix well with a fork.

4 Fill each muffin cup to the top with potato mixture.
Sprinkle remaining shredded cheese on each muffin cup.

5 Bake for 10-15 minutes until golden brown.
Let cool in pan for 5 minutes before removing patties.

Nutrition Snapshot
Per mini-patty: 63 calories, 3g fat, 2g saturated fat, 3g protein,
6g carbs, 1g fiber, 1g sugar, 149mg sodium

Greek Bean Salad

1 cup frozen or fresh haricots verts (French green beans), cooked

½ cup canned garbanzo beans, rinsed and drained

½ (12-oz) jar **Giant White Beans** (not rinsed or drained)

⅓ cup onion, minced

1 cup **Medley Seedless Grapes**, halved, or any combination of grapes

⅓ cup feta cheese, crumbled

Vinaigrette

2 Tbsp olive oil

1 tsp white balsamic vinegar

Juice of ½ lemon

Pinch salt and pepper

Prep time 10 minutes
Serves 2

1 Place haricots verts, beans, onion, grapes, and feta in large bowl.

2 In a small bowl, whisk vinaigrette ingredients.
Pour vinaigrette on salad and toss to coat. Chill and marinate overnight.

Note

The longer this salad marinates, the better it tastes.

Helpful Tip

Beans are a delicious, comforting, and economical way to feed your family. They are a great source of fiber, protein, calcium, iron, folic acid, and potassium, as well as being low in fat. Cooked beans keep up to four or five days in the fridge and freeze well. Make a pot of beans once a week, or make extra for a particular recipe, so that you have cooked beans on hand.

Nutrition Snapshot

Per serving: 626 calories, 21g fat, 6g saturated fat, 30g protein, 86g carbs, 19g fiber, 21g sugar, 476mg sodium

White Bean Soup

2 cups leftover cooked (or canned) white kidney beans

3 Tbsp olive oil, divided

½ cup onion, minced

1 clove garlic, minced, or 1 cube frozen **Crushed Garlic**

1 bay leaf

3 cups chicken or vegetable broth

¼ cup heavy cream

2 Tofurky soy sausages or other sausage

Prep and cooking time 25 minutes

Hands-off cooking time 10 minutes

Makes 5 (1-cup servings)

1 Heat olive oil in a soup pot over medium-high heat.
Add onion and garlic; cook and stir for 7-8 minutes until onion is soft and transparent.
Add bay leaf and beans; stir to combine.

2 Add broth and increase heat, bringing to a boil.
Simmer for 10 minutes. Discard bay leaf.

3 Purée soup with an immersion blender, or blend soup in batches with a blender.
Add cream and mix well.

4 In a saucepan, cook sausages in 1 Tbsp olive oil until brown.
Let cool until safe to handle, and crumble sausage into soup.

Note
See Safety Tip on p. 52

Nutrition Snapshot
Per serving: 275 calories, 16g fat, 6g saturated fat, 13g protein, 21g carbs, 10g fiber, 2g sugar, 631mg sodium

Lentil Salad with Pancetta and Andouille

½ (17.6-oz) pkg refrigerated **Steamed Lentils**

2 Tbsp olive oil

½ (14.5 oz) container refrigerated **Mirepoix**
or ½ cup each celery, carrots, and onion

1 tsp finely chopped fresh thyme

1 bay leaf

Salt to taste

½ (4-oz) container **Pancetta Cubetti** (pancetta mini-cubes)

2 **Andouille Chicken Sausages**, cut in ½-inch slices

Vinaigrette

1 Tbsp red wine vinegar

½ Tbsp Dijon mustard

Salt and pepper to taste

2 Tbsp olive oil

Prep and cooking time 30 minutes
Serves 4

1 Add oil to a 12-inch skillet over medium-low heat. Add mirepoix, thyme, bay leaf, salt, and pepper; cook and stir occasionally until vegetables are tender, about 10-12 minutes. Add pancetta and cook for 5 minutes more. Add sausages and cook for 5 minutes more. Remove from heat and set aside.

2 In a small bowl, whisk vinegar, mustard, salt, and pepper. Add olive oil and whisk to emulsify.

3 Add lentils and vinaigrette to the still-warm vegetable mixture and toss to coat. Discard bay leaf. Eat warm, cold, or at room temperature.

Nutrition Snapshot

*Per serving: 329 calories, 22g fat, 4g saturated fat, 20g protein,
15g carbs, 6g fiber, 4g sugar, 751mg sodium*

Pasta e Fagioli

1 ½ cups cooked leftover or canned pinto beans

½ (14.5-oz) container **Mirepoix** or ½ cup each celery, carrot, and onion

1 clove garlic, minced, or 1 cube frozen **Crushed Garlic**

2 Tbsp olive oil

5 cups low-sodium chicken broth, vegetable broth, or water

⅓ cup **Traditional Marinara Sauce** or your favorite marinara

Salt and pepper to taste

1 cup penne pasta

1 Tbsp fresh parsley

Prep and cooking time 20 minutes

Makes 5 (1-cup) servings

1 In a saucepan over medium heat, cook and stir mirepoix and garlic in oil for 7-10 minutes until onion is soft and transparent.

2 Add broth, marinara, salt, and pepper. Bring to a boil.

3 Add pasta and simmer until pasta is cooked. Stir in beans.

4 If using low-sodium broth, taste soup and season with salt and pepper. Add water if too thick. Stir in parsley.

Nutrition Snapshot

Per serving: 200 calories, 7g fat, 1g saturated fat, 8g protein, 26g carbs, 6g fiber, 5g sugar, 412mg sodium

Indian Lentil Pâté

1 cup refrigerated **Steamed Lentils** or leftover lentils

⅓ cup refrigerated **Mirepoix** or 2 Tbsp each chopped celery, carrot, and onion

1 trimmed leek

3 Tbsp olive oil

Pinch salt and pepper

3 eggs

4 Tbsp jarred **Thai Yellow Curry Sauce**

½ cup cooked quinoa

Prep time 10 minutes
Hands-off
cooking time 30-35 minutes
Serves 4

1 Preheat oven to 375°F.

2 In a food processor, finely chop mirepoix and leek.

3 In a medium skillet, heat olive oil and cook mirepoix-leek mixture for 10 minutes, stirring occasionally. Add salt and pepper.

4 Beat eggs in a large bowl, then add mirepoix-leek mixture, lentils, curry sauce, and quinoa. Mix well.

5 Generously oil a standard loaf pan and pour batter into it. Bake for 30-35 minutes or until pâté is firm and golden. Let cool completely in pan before slicing.

Nutrition Snapshot
Per serving: 292 calories, 17g fat, 3g saturated fat, 9g protein, 26g carbs, 4g fiber, 3g sugar, 357mg sodium

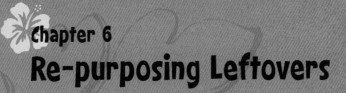

Chapter 6
Re-purposing Leftovers

Pasta, Breads and Grains

Pasta Pie

2 cups cooked spaghetti or angel hair pasta

½ cup ricotta cheese

¾ cup **Shredded 3 Cheese Blend**

3 slices **Italian coppa**, shredded

3 slices **Calabrese Salami**, shredded

4 eggs, beaten

Pinch salt and pepper

1 tsp fresh thyme

Prep time 10 minutes

Hands-off cooking time 20 minutes

Serves 6

  * Substitute Tofurky Deli meatless slices.

1 Preheat oven to 375°F.

2 In a large bowl, mix ricotta, shredded cheese, copa, salami, eggs, salt, pepper, and thyme. Add pasta and mix well.

3 Lightly oil a deep 9-inch pie pan. Pour pasta mixture into pie pan.

4 Bake for 20 minutes or until top is brown and pie is set.

5 Let cool slightly before cutting into wedges. Eat warm, cold, or at room temperature.

Note

Coppa is an Italian cured deli meat. The **Volpi Trio** *package at Trader Joe's comes with mortadella, Genova salame, and coppa. Substitute any type of salami, prosciutto, or ham.*

Nutrition Snapshot

Per serving: 211 calories, 10g fat, 5g saturated fat, 14g protein, 15g carbs, 1g fiber, 1g sugar, 371mg sodium

Tri-Color Pasta Salad

2 cups cooked **Vegetable Radiatore** (tri-color) pasta

3 slices **Calabrese salame**, shredded

3 slices **Capocollo,** shredded

⅓ cup **Julienne Sliced Sun Dried Tomatoes in Olive Oil**, drained

⅓ cup toasted pine nuts

⅓ cup chopped **Stuffed Queen Sevillano Olives**

2 Tbsp olive oil

1 Tbsp white balsamic vinegar

Pinch salt and pepper

Prep time 10 minutes

Serves 4

  * Substitute Tofurky Deli meatless slices.

1 In a large bowl, mix pasta, cold cuts, sun dried tomato, pine nuts, and olives.

2 Gently toss with oil, vinegar, salt, and pepper.

Note
Capocollo is an Italian cured deli meat. The Gourmet Deli Selection package at Trader Joe's comes with 3 cured meats: Calabrese salame, prosciutto, and capocollo. Substitute any type of salami, prosciutto, or ham.

Nutrition Snapshot
Per serving: 303 calories, 20g fat, 2g saturated fat, 8g protein, 23g carbs, 2g fiber, 2g sugar, 482mg sodium

Mâche Ado About Lentil Salad

1 cup cooked **Lemon Pepper or Egg Pappardelle** pasta

1-2 cloves garlic, minced, or 1-2 cubes frozen **Crushed Garlic**

2 cups mâche (lamb's lettuce)

¼ cup refrigerated **Steamed Lentils**

1 Tbsp olive oil

2 tsp balsamic vinegar

Salt and freshly ground black pepper, to taste

2 oz **Truffle Italian Cheese** or Swiss cheese, cut into thin ribbons

Prep time 10 minutes
Serves 2

1 In a large bowl, mix pasta and garlic. Stir in mâche, lentils, oil, and vinegar.
   Adjust seasonings if desired.

2 Add cheese on top.

Nutrition Snapshot
*Per serving: 334 calories, 16g fat, 7g saturated fat, 13g protein,
32g carbs, 5g fiber, 3g sugar, 496mg sodium*

Lemony Garlic Penne with Zucchini and Ricotta

2 cups cooked penne pasta

3 Tbsp olive oil, divided

4 small organic zucchini (12 oz), peeled into ribbons with a vegetable peeler

Pinch salt and pepper

1-2 cloves garlic, minced, or 1-2 cubes frozen **Crushed Garlic**

2 tsp fresh lemon juice

Zest of 1 organic lemon

4 oz ricotta cheese

Prep and cooking time 20 minutes

Serves 2

1 Heat 2 Tbsp oil in a saucepan over medium heat. Add zucchini ribbons, salt, and pepper and sauté 5 minutes or until tender. Add garlic and cook for 1 minute more.

2 In a large bowl, combine cooked zucchini ribbons, lemon juice, lemon zest, and remaining oil. Add pasta and mix gently.

3 Add ricotta cheese on top.

Helpful Tip

We have pasta night once a week in our home. Since it doesn't take any longer to cook, I cook double the amount of pasta I need and keep leftovers in the fridge, handy for creating a quick lunch during the week to come. Add chicken, ham, tomato, fresh herbs, or any vegetables you have on hand, toss with vinaigrette, and create a nutritious pasta salad in minutes.

Nutrition Snapshot

Per serving: 505 calories, 26g fat, 6g saturated fat, 15g protein, 54g carbs, 5g fiber, 7g sugar, 172mg sodium

Parisian Salad

⅓ cup canned or frozen corn kennels

1 (8-oz) pkg refrigerated **Steamed and Peeled Baby Beets**, thinly sliced

1 large hard-boiled egg, peeled and cut in wedges

⅓ cup cooked or canned garbanzo beans, rinsed and drained

⅓ cup cooked or canned kidney beans, rinsed and drained

½ English cucumber, peeled and sliced

2 small tomatoes, cut in wedges

3 slices **Healthy Cooked ham** or **Rosemary Ham**, cut in ½ inch strips

2 oz **French Abbaye Ste Mere** cheese or Swiss cheese, cut into ½-inch cubes

Salt and pepper to taste

Vinaigrette

⅛ tsp salt

¼ tsp black pepper

1 Tbsp red wine vinegar

½ small shallot, peeled and minced

½ teaspoon Dijon mustard

2 Tbsp olive oil

Prep time 10 minutes

Serves 4

 *Omit ham

1 In a small bowl, mix all vinaigrette ingredients except oil.
Slowly add oil and whisk. If vinaigrette is too sharp, add additional olive oil.

2 In a large bowl, mix remaining ingredients. Pour vinaigrette over salad and toss to coat.

Nutrition Snapshot

Per serving: 445 calories, 25g fat, 8g saturated fat, 24g protein,
31g carbs, 7g fiber, 16g sugar, 745mg sodium

Butternut Squash & Feta Green Salad

½ (12-oz) bag **Cut Butternut Squash** (2 cups cubed butternut squash), cooked

½ cup canned garbanzo beans, rinsed and drained

½ cup canned kidney beans, rinsed and drained

1 Tbsp diced onion

1 cup **Organics Spring Mix**

1 tsp fresh thyme

⅛ tsp salt

¼ tsp black pepper

¼ cup **Crumbled Feta** (or crumble your own feta)

Dressing

1 Tbsp mayonnaise

1 Tbsp plain yogurt

1 Tbsp olive oil

1 tsp lemon juice

⅛ tsp salt

⅛ tsp black pepper

Prep time 10 minutes
Serves 2

1   Combine butternut squash, beans, onion, salad, and thyme in a mixing bowl. Sprinkle with salt and pepper. Sprinkle feta on top of salad.

2   In a small bowl, whisk dressing ingredients. Pour dressing on salad and toss gently.

Nutrition Snapshot

Per serving: 304 calories, 13g fat, 3g saturated fat, 18g protein, 37g carbs, 7g fiber, 12g sugar, 772mg sodium

Provençal Bread Soup

2 slices stale ciabatta bread, each 1-2 inches thick

1 whole clove garlic, cut in half

¼ cup olive oil

1 clove garlic, minced, or 1 cube frozen **Crushed Garlic**

2 large fresh basil leaves, washed and sliced into narrow strips

1 cup jarred **Traditional Marinara Sauce** or your favorite marinara sauce

1 cup frozen **Fire Roasted Bell Pepper and Onion**, thawed

2 cups vegetable broth, chicken broth, or water

Salt and pepper to taste

Pinch 21 **Salute Seasoning**

Prep time
15 minutes + 10 minutes soak time
Cooking time 25 minutes
Serves 3

1 Toast bread in toaster. While still hot, rub each side of bread with garlic clove halves. Break bread into small 1-inch pieces. Set aside.

2 In a medium saucepan, heat oil over medium heat. Add bell pepper-onion mix. Cook and stir for 5 minutes. Add garlic and basil and cook for 1 additional minute.

3 Stir in marinara and bring to a boil on medium-high heat.

4 Return to a boil, reduce heat, cover, and simmer for 10-15 minutes, stirring frequently and breaking up bread with the back of a spoon. The bread should break down to a mush, thickening the soup. Sprinkle with 21 Seasoning Salute.
If using low-sodium broth, taste soup and season with salt and pepper.

Nutrition Snapshot
Per serving: 363 calories, 20g fat, 3g saturated fat, 7g protein,
44g carbs, 5g fiber, 12g sugar, 666mg sodium

Garbanzo Panzanella Salad

2 slices day-old **Filone or Ciabata** bread, 2 inches thick

1 whole garlic clove, cut in half

3 Tbsp olive oil, divided

1 (15-oz) can garbanzo beans, rinsed and drained

2 small tomatoes, sliced

1 (6-oz) can white tuna in olive oil, drained

1 small white or red onion, thinly sliced

1 Tbsp red wine vinegar

Salt to taste

½ tsp black pepper

Prep time 15 minutes

Serves 2

1 Toast bread in toaster. While still hot, rub bread with garlic, then brush bread with 2 tsp oil. Tear into 1- or 2-inch pieces.

2 In a large bowl, combine bread, beans, tomatoes, tuna, onion, vinegar, remaining oil, salt, and pepper. Mix well to blend flavors.

Note
The longer the salad stays, the better it tastes; can be made the day before.

Nutrition Snapshot
Per serving: 661 calories, 29g fat, 4g saturated fat, 36g protein, 65g carbs, 10g fiber, 3g sugar, 1,114mg sodium

Jammin' Ricotta Bites

1 cup of stale sandwich bread (with or without crust), cut into bite-size pieces

2 small eggs, beaten

½ cup low-fat (2 %) milk

⅓ cup ricotta or cream cheese

⅓ cup **Organic Reduced Sugar Strawberry Preserves**

Prep time 10 minutes
Hands-off cooking time 12-17 minutes
Makes 12 bites

1 Preheat oven to 375°F.

2 Butter or lightly oil a 12-cup mini muffin pan.

3 In a medium bowl, mix eggs and milk. Set aside.

4 Place bread pieces into muffin cups, filling ¾ full. Lightly compact bread with your fingers.

5 Add ½ tsp ricotta cheese to muffin cup, then pour 1 Tbsp egg mixture on top.

6 Top with ½ tsp jam in each muffin cup.

7 Bake for 12-17 minutes until golden.

8 Let cool in pan for about 5 minutes before removing from cups.

Nutrition Snapshot

Per bite: 46 calories, 2g fat, 1g saturated fat, 2g protein, 5g carbs, 0g fiber, 3g sugar, 43mg sodium

Chocolate and Almond Bread Pudding Muffins

2 ½ cups stale sandwich bread
(with or without crust), cut into bite-size pieces

2 eggs, beaten

⅓ cup milk

¼ cup heavy cream

⅓ cup unsweetened cocoa powder

1 tsp vanilla extract

⅓ cup sugar

½ cup sliced almonds

⅓ cup semi-sweet chocolate chips

Prep time 15 minutes
Hands-off
cooking time 15-20 minutes
Makes 6 muffins

1 Preheat oven to 375°F.

2 Butter or lightly oil a standard muffin pan.

3 In a medium bowl, mix eggs, milk, cream, cocoa, vanilla, and sugar.

4 Cover bottom of 6 muffin cups with bread. Lightly compact with your fingers.
Portion egg mixture into muffin cups, filling almost to the top.
Sprinkle with almonds and chocolate chips.

5 Bake for 15-20 minutes until golden brown.
Let cool in pan for 5 minutes before removing from muffin pan.

Nutrition Snapshot

Per muffin: 273 calories, 14g fat, 8g saturated fat, 7g protein,
32g carbs, 4g fiber, 20g sugar, 130mg sodium

Crispy Cinnamon Bread

4 slices sandwich bread

2 tsp cinnamon

1 Tbsp sugar

⅓ cup melted unsalted butter

Prep time 15 minutes
Hands-off
cooking time 12-17 minutes
Serves 4

1 Preheat oven to 375°F.

2 In a small bowl, mix cinnamon and sugar.

3 Use cookie cutters to cut shapes out of sandwich bread.

4 Brush each shaped bread with melted butter on one side only.

5 Sprinkle with cinnamon-sugar mixture.

6 Place on a baking sheet and bake for 12-17 minutes until golden.
Let cool for 5 minutes on a rack.

Note

Kids love to make these! A toaster oven makes it quick and easy to prepare. Any shape or size of cookie cutter can be used, but kids love flowers, hearts, and animal shapes.

Nutrition Snapshot

Per serving: 180 calories, 15g fat, 11g saturated fat, 1g protein, 10g carbs, 1g fiber, 7g sugar, 83mg sodium

French Picnic Rice Salad

3 cups cooked Basmati rice or any long grain rice

2 Tbsp olive oil

2 cups frozen **Fire Roasted Bell Peppers and Onions**

1 cup frozen **Organic Foursome**

Pinch salt and pepper

1 large tomato, chopped

½ cup green olives, chopped

2 hard-boiled eggs, peeled and cut in wedges

Vinaigrette

¼ cup olive oil

3 Tbsp red wine vinegar

1-2 tsp Dijon mustard

Salt and pepper to taste

Prep time 15 minutes
Hands-off cooking time 10 minutes
Serves 6

1   Heat a saucepan with olive oil over medium heat. Add pepper-onion mix (no need to thaw), and cook and stir for 3 minutes. Add Organic Foursome mix (no need to thaw) and cook for 7-10 minutes longer until all vegetables are soft. Season with salt and pepper.

2   In a salad bowl, combine rice, vegetable mixture, tomato, olives, and eggs.

3   In a small bowl, whisk vinaigrette ingredients. Pour dressing over rice mixture. Adjust seasoning if needed. Refrigerate.

Nutrition Snapshot

Per serving: 347 calories, 17g fat, 3g saturated fat, 7g protein, 45g carbs, 6g fiber, 14g sugar, 279mg sodium

Colorful Lemon Quinoa

2 cups cooked quinoa

10 cherry tomatoes, halved

½ cup chopped cucumber, seeded and diced

2 Tbsp chopped cilantro

1 Tbsp minced onion

¼ cup chopped hazelnuts

Pomegranate seeds for garnish

Lemon zest for garnish

Vinaigrette

3 Tbsp olive oil

1 Tbsp white balsamic vinegar

1 tsp fresh lemon juice

1 tsp organic lemon zest,
plus additional for garnish

Pinch salt and pepper

Prep time 10 minutes
Serves 5

1 In a large bowl, mix quinoa, tomatoes, cucumber, cilantro, onion, and hazelnuts.

2 In a small bowl, whisk vinaigrette ingredients. Pour vinaigrette over quinoa mixture and stir to coat. Garnish with lemon zest and pomegranate seeds. Serve at room temperature or cold.

Nutrition Snapshot

*Per serving: 217 calories, 13g fat, 1g saturated fat, 5g protein,
22g carbs, 2g fiber, 2g sugar, 43mg sodium*

Easy Jambalaya

1 cup cooked white rice

1 (6-8 oz) chicken breast, cut in ½-inch strips

½ tsp salt

½ tsp black pepper

2 Tbsp olive oil

1 cup **Mirepoix**, or ⅓ cup each chopped celery, onion, and carrot

1 clove garlic, minced, or 1 cube frozen **Crushed Garlic**

2 smoked **Chicken Andouille Sausages**, cut into ½-inch slices

1 cup frozen **Fire Roasted Bell Pepper and Onions**

1 cup frozen cooked shrimp, thawed

1 tsp chopped fresh cilantro

Prep and cooking time
30 minutes
Serves 6

1 Season chicken on both sides with salt and pepper.

2 Heat oil in a large, deep skillet over high heat and cook chicken for 6-10 minutes, flipping halfway through, until browned and cooked. Remove and drain on paper towel. Set aside.

3 To the same saucepan over medium heat, add mirepoix, garlic, sausage, pepper-onion mix, and shrimp. Cook and stir for 8-12 minutes.

4 Add rice. Reduce heat to medium-low and cook, stirring occasionally, for 3 minutes.

5 Sprinkle with cilantro. Toss well.

Did you know?
It is true that brown rice has more calcium, iron, fiber, and protein than white rice, but brown rice is less digestible than white rice. So if you prefer white rice, eat it with lots of beans or vegetables.

Nutrition Snapshot
Per serving: 247 calories, 9g fat, 2g saturated fat, 21g protein, 21g carbs, 4g fiber, 7g sugar, 681mg sodium

California Sunshine Quinoa Salad

1 cup cooked quinoa

⅓ cup golden raisins

2 oranges peeled and sliced

4 Medjool dates, pitted and coarsely chopped

⅓ cup raw sliced almonds

1 tsp ground cinnamon

Dressing
Juice of 1 orange

⅓ cup honey

1 tsp olive oil

Salt to taste

Prep time 5 minutes
Serves 4

1   In a large bowl, combine quinoa, raisins, oranges, dates, and almonds. Set aside

2   In a small bowl, whisk dressing ingredients. Pour dressing over quinoa mixture.
    Sprinkle with cinnamon and mix again. Eat cold or at room temperature.

Nutrition Snapshot
*Per serving: 330 calories, 6g fat, 0g saturated fat, 6g protein,
72g carbs, 6g fiber, 51g sugar, 5mg sodium*

Green Herbed Couscous

1 cup cooked whole wheat couscous

1 small avocado

Juice of ½ lemon, divided

1 Tbsp minced onion

¼ cup chopped cilantro

2 ½ Tbsp chopped fresh mint leaves

1 Tbsp chopped fresh parsley leaves

1 Tbsp chopped fresh oregano leaves

2 Tbsp olive oil

2 tsp white balsamic vinegar

Salt and pepper to taste

Prep time 10 minutes
Serves 4

1 Cut avocado in tiny pieces and sprinkle with ½ tsp lemon juice.

2 In a large bowl, mix couscous, onion, herbs, oil, vinegar, remaining lemon juice, salt, pepper, and avocado. Adjust seasonings. Eat cold or at room temperature.

Nutrition Snapshot

Per serving: 159 calories, 12g fat, 2g saturated fat, 3g protein, 16g carbs, 4g fiber, 1g sugar, 9mg sodium

Chapter 7

Ready-made
Snacks

Trader Joe's has a wide selection of ready-to-eat items that are useful as lunchbox add-ons and between-meal snacks. Trader Joe's has the traditional snack standbys, such as baby carrots and string cheese, but they also offer a broader selection of convenience snacks, perfect for stuffing into backpacks or taking along on an outing. Some of my favorites are included here:

Fruits & Vegetables

Pre-cut fruit. Whole fruit is always a great snack, but peeled or sliced fruit adds variety without extra effort. Trader Joe's sells apples, pineapple, melon, mango, and other fruit in season, pre-cut and ready to go.

Fresh vegetables. In addition to the standard carrot sticks and celery sticks, try assortments of crisp cauliflower florets, bell pepper strips, Persian cucumbers, edamame, or sugar snap peas. All are tasty raw and require little prep.

Avocados. Trader Joe's always has bags of affordable avocados, available organic or conventionally grown. Avocados are a source of healthy fats and they come in their own convenient take-along packaging. Serve avocado halves with a spoon, and drizzle with a squeeze of lemon juice (just enough to coat) to keep it from turning brown.

Freeze-dried fruit. Freeze-dried fruit offers a light crunchiness that everyone loves, especially kids. Enjoy exotic selections such as mangosteen and rambutan, as well as mango, banana, and strawberry.

Natural fruit leather. This chewy snack doubles as dessert for those who like to finish a meal with something sweet and fruity.

Freeze-dried vegetables. Green beans are dried until crisp and offer a satisfying crunchiness. Older kids and adults may enjoy wasabi peas. It's hard to eat just one!

Snapea Crisps. This snack is made of pureed peas and is an alternative to potato chips. They can also be tossed in a green salad, like croutons.

Roasted Seaweed Snack. You either love 'em or hate 'em. These paper thin, crispy sheets of dried seaweed have been a hit since they appeared on store shelves.

Grains

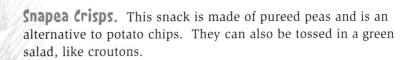

Trader Joe's **100-calorie packs** of crackers and cookies are a small and convenient snack portion for kids as well as grown-ups who are watching their waistlines.

Trader Joe's many varieties of **granola bars** includes the wholesome Five Seed Almond Bar which features flax seeds, almond meal and even fish oil! But you'd never know with this bar that tastes like a cookie, sweetened with pureed raisins.

Yogurt-covered pretzels and **peanut-butter-filled pretzels.** Trader Joe's more natural and more affordable versions of these sweet and salty snacks are a favorite.

Rice cakes. Available in brown rice or regular rice varieties, these light and crisp creations are great on their own, or with hummus, peanut butter, or slices of cheese.

Whole grain chips. At Trader Joe's, you can find many variations including flax seed tortilla chips, hemp seed chips, and lentil chips.

Honey wheat pretzels. With just a touch of honey, these pretzel sticks are a favorite of kids everywhere. Enjoy as is, or dip into nut butters or yogurt.

Mini muffins. Available in the bakery section, these treats are just the right size for lunchboxes and mid-day snacks. Try making your own using Trader Joe's many muffin mixes and a miniature-size muffin pan.

Protein

Trail mix. Choose among an extensive selection of ready-to-go trail mix, or make your own by mixing your favorite dried fruits and nuts. Not only are the fruits and nuts at TJ's affordable, but their high turnover assures that you'll be getting fresh product, never stale or rancid.

Nuts. Nuts are chock full of protein, trace minerals, and healthy oils. Trader Joe's sells single-serving "Just a Handful" packs of almonds (raw or roasted), cashews, and trail mix, which are easy to toss into a bag, purse, or backpack.

Yogurt cups and yogurt squeezers. Pack these portable yogurts with small ice packs or the mini zippered insulated cases that are used for soft drinks.

Sausages. Trader Joe's sausages are a lower-sodium and nitrate-free alternative to traditional hot dogs. Slice them into shapes or sticks for kids and pack them along with cheese sticks and crackers.

All-natural beef jerky and turkey jerky. This high protein, low-fat, minimally processed snack is stable at room temperature and easy to pack. It is made with organic meat raised without hormones and antibiotics, and has no preservatives, gluten, msg, nitrites, or artificial ingredients.

Cheese sticks, wedges, wheels, or spreads. Trader Joe's has an extensive cheese selection to satisfy the most discerning of palates. Mix it up and alternate flavors, shapes, and textures throughout the week.

Hummus. Trader Joe's selection of hummus will made anyone's head spin – variations include bean hummus, eggplant hummus, edamame hummus, and a symphony of regular chickpea hummus. Include baby carrots, fresh snap peas, Persian cucumber slices, and crackers to dip and eat.

Ready-to-eat steamed edamame. Eat these little tasty treats plain as a snack, as part of a bento, or mixed in with rice or other veggies. They come in the pod or already shelled.

Any of these snacks are great on their own. For a more substantial and balanced snack, combine one snack item from each category using the following rule of thumb:

1 fruit or vegetable + 1 grains + 1 protein

Fruit/Vegetables	✚ Grains	✚ Protein
Apples	Rice crackers	Cheese stick or slices
Freeze dried green beans	Pretzel sticks	Cashews
Carrots, bell peppers	Pita bread or chips	Hummus
Dried mango slices	Flax seed tortilla chips	Yogurt squeezer tube
Avocado	5-seed almond bar	Turkey jerky
Fresh berries	Kashi crackers	Mini Babybel cheese

These are examples.

Chapter 8

Snacks, Desserts and Sweets

Savory Cookies

For pre-dinner drinks or aperitif we often wrap bacon around prunes and bake until the bacon is crispy. This perfectly paired sweet-salty treat provides the inspiration for savory cookies. These grab-and-go crispy cookies are perfect to snack on in the afternoon when you are craving something salty and crunchy.

3 slices bacon, preferably Applewood uncured bacon

3 oz **Pitted Dried Prunes**, chopped

1 cup **Shredded 3 Cheese Blend**

1 cup all-purpose flour

2 Tbsp olive oil

¼ tsp salt

Pinch black pepper

Prep and cooking time 15 minutes
Hands-off cooking time 20 minutes
Makes 10 cookies

1 Preheat oven to 350°F.

2 Cut bacon into small strips (kitchen shears are helpful). In a skilled (with no oil), cook bacon until crispy. Drain on paper towel.

3 In a large bowl, mix bacon, prunes, cheese, flour, olive oil, salt, and pepper. Mix until the consistency of cookie dough. Add water if dough is too dry.

4 Drop dough in spoonfuls, 1 inch apart, onto oiled or parchment-paper-lined baking sheet. Flatten cookies with the back of a spoon.

5 Bake for 15-20 minutes until golden. Once cookies cool, store in an airtight container.

Nutrition Snapshot
Per cookie: 135 calories, 7g fat, 3g saturated fat, 5g protein, 13g carbs, 1g fiber, 2g sugar, 173mg sodium

Tiny Tartes Tatin

Tarte tatin is the quintessential French upside-down apple caramel pie. This easy version creates cute individual tarts, making it just as appropriate for portable lunches as for an elegant dinner. I skip the tricky preparation of caramel sauce by using Trader Joe's delicious Fleur de Sel Caramel Sauce, smooth and sweet with just a hint of salt.

1 frozen pie crust, thawed but still cold

4 tsp jarred **Fleur de Sel Caramel Sauce**

4 small Fuji apples or other firm apple

Juice of 1 lemon

2 Tbsp butter

2 tsp sugar

Prep time 20 minutes

Hands-off cooking time 25 minutes

Makes 4 individual tarts

1 Preheat oven to 375°F.

2 Lay crust on a lightly floured surface without stretching it. Use 4-inch tart pans with removable bottoms as cookie cutters and cut four tarts. Set aside; do not place crust into tart pans yet. Pour 1 tsp caramel into bottoms of each tart pan. Set aside.

3 Peel, core, and slice apples very thinly, and toss with lemon juice in a bowl.

4 Melt butter in a saucepan over medium heat. Add apple slices; gently cook and stir until apples are coated, about 5 minutes. Sprinkle with sugar and cook until tender and golden. Set aside to cool slightly.

5 Place apple slices in overlapping patterns on top of caramel-covered tart pans. Top with crusts cut earlier. Tuck edges of crust down inside tart pans. Place tart pans on a cookie sheet or baking pan to catch caramel drippings.

6 Bake tarts on center rack for 12-16 minutes. Allow tarts to cool for 5 minutes, then invert and remove from pans when still warm.
If caramel cools too much and hardens, tarts will be difficult to remove.

Nutrition Snapshot

Per tart: 306 calories, 17g fat, 6g saturated fat, 2g protein, 38g carbs, 3g fiber, 17g sugar, 231mg sodium

Gâteau au Yogurt (Yogurt Cake)

Yogurt cake or gâteau au yaourt *is a classic cake in France. It was the first cake I baked as a child, using an empty plastic yogurt cup to measure ingredients. This cake is delicious as-is, but you can add anything you like to the batter: coconut flakes, lemon or orange peels, or chocolate chips are some ideas. Serve slices with jam or drizzled with Fleur de Sel Caramel Sauce.*

1 cup plain whole milk yogurt, such as plain Cream Line Yogurt

2 large eggs

1 cup sugar

1 tsp vanilla extract

⅓ cup vegetable oil

2 cups all-purpose flour

1 ½ tsp baking powder

Pinch salt

Prep time 10 minutes
Hands-off cooking time 35 minutes
Serves 8

1 Preheat oven to 350°F.

2 Lightly oil and flour an 8-inch or 9-inch round or square cake pan.

3 In a large mixing bowl, combine yogurt, eggs, sugar, vanilla, and oil. In another bowl, sift flour, baking powder, and salt. Add flour mixture to yogurt mixture, and mix until smooth. Pour batter into prepared cake pan.

4 Bake for 30-35 minutes until top is golden brown and knife inserted near center comes out clean. Let stand for 10 minutes, then transfer onto a rack to let cool.

Nutrition Snapshot

Per serving: 330 calories, 12g fat, 2g saturated fat, 6g protein, 50g carbs, 1g fiber, 27g sugar, 145mg sodium

Mahalo Fruit Salad

I am always wondering why people buy canned fruit instead of making their own fruit salad. Fruit salad is a simple, fast, low-calorie dessert that is packed with nutrients – from minerals to antioxidants, vitamins, and hundreds of phytochemicals. Don't neglect all the fruits in the fridge or fruit bowl. Be creative and make an irresistible, colorful salad. This tropical fruit salad is great during winter months when domestic fruits are not their best. If desired, drizzle with honey, agave nectar, or even yogurt!

1 (16-oz) pkg refrigerated **Tropical Fruit Medley**
(mango, pineapple, and papaya)

Juice of 1 orange

1 cup blueberries

½ cup pomegranate seeds

Prep Time 5 minutes
Serves 1

1   Cut the fruits into bite size pieces and place in a large bowl. Pour juice and mix well.

2   Add blueberries and pomegranate seeds. Keep refrigerated.

Nutrition Snapshot
Per serving: 341 calories, 2g fat, 0g saturated fat, 6g protein, 104g carbs, 13g fiber, 78g sugar, 2mg sodium

Tropical Fruit Kebabs

Fruit kebabs are fun to make and to eat. Use a variety of firm fruits, such as melons, pineapple, and berries, stringing them together with wooden skewers. You can either follow a single color theme (strawberries and watermelon) or create a multi-colored rainbow kebab. Kids enjoy making them, so let them do the work! (Make sure to trim sharp ends of skewers with scissors for younger children.) Drizzle kebabs with honey, if desired, or dip into yogurt.

1 slice papaya, 1 slice mango, and 4 pieces pineapple
(from refrigerated **Tropical Fruit Medley**)

6 blueberries

2 bamboo skewers

Prep Time 5 minutes
Makes 2 Kebabs

1   Cut papaya and mango slices into bite size pieces. Thread all fruits with a stick.

2   Wrap in plastic wrap and chill until time to eat. Serve with yogurt dipping sauce or Fleur de Sel Caramel Sauce.

Nutrition Snapshot
Per kebab: 47 calories, 0g fat, 0g saturated fat, 1g protein, 12g carbs, 2g fiber, 9g sugar, 1mg sodium

Apple Mini Cakes

My family enjoys these soft and moist little apple cakes, full of autumn flavors, for brunch or goûter (afternoon snack time). I like to place these little apple cakes in my kids' snack bag without saying anything. I imagine them talking to their friends and laughing as they open their bag to discover a great snack, and it makes me smile. For presentation at home, press an apple slice into the tops of each cake and drizzle with Trader Joe's Fleur de Sel Caramel Sauce.

4 small Fuji apples, peeled

⅔ cup plus 1 Tbsp butter, softened

1 cup plus 1 Tbsp sugar

2 eggs

1 tsp vanilla extract

1 ½ cups flour

1 ½ tsp baking powder

Pinch salt

Prep time 20 minutes
Hand-off cooking time 13-18 minutes
Makes 12 mini cakes

1 Preheat oven to 375°F. Lightly oil and flour a 12-cup standard muffin pan or line with paper baking cups.

2 Grate apples and add to a saucepan with 1 Tbsp butter and 1 Tbsp sugar. Stir and cook over medium heat for 8 minutes. Set aside to cool.

3 Meanwhile, cream 1 cup sugar and ⅔ cup softened butter. Add eggs and vanilla extract. Mix well. Fold in flour, baking powder, and salt.

4 Fold sautéed apples into batter. Portion batter into muffin cups, ⅔ full.

5 Bake for 13-18 minutes or until a toothpick inserted near center comes out clean.

6 Remove from oven and let cool in pans on cooling racks for 10 minutes before removing muffins.

Nutrition Snapshot
Per mini cake: 264 calories, 13g fat, 8g saturated fat, 2g protein, 35g carbs, 1g fiber, 22g sugar, 189mg sodium

Homemade Almond Croissants

These are my husband's favorite sweet treat – something he always loved getting at bakeries in France. I made them on a Sunday morning out of the blue, and he was so happy to discover them on the kitchen counter. These croissants are very rich, so you may consider eating one half and sharing the other.

6 stale croissants
⅓ cup plus 3 Tbsp sugar
1 cup water
1 cup Just Almond Meal
Pinch salt
½ cup unsalted butter, softened
2 large eggs
Powdered sugar for garnish

Prep time 15 minutes
Hands-off cooking time 15-20 minutes
Makes 6 croissants

1   Preheat oven to 350°F.

2   In a medium saucepan, combine 3 Tbsp sugar and water. Bring to a boil over medium heat, simmer for 2 minutes, stirring well, and then let cool. Set this syrup aside.

3   In a large bowl, combine almond meal, remaining sugar, salt, and butter. Mix until blended. Add eggs one by one, stirring well after each addition.

4   Slice croissants in half lengthwise. Using a brush, generously moisten croissants (inside and out) with water-sugar syrup.

5   Place croissant bottoms on oiled or parchment-paper-lined cookie sheet. Divide almond mixture among croissant bottoms, spreading gently with a spoon. Put tops back on.

6   Bake for 15-20 minutes until golden. Remove from oven and dust with powdered sugar before serving.

Nutrition Snapshot
Per croissant: 507 calories,
31g fat, 13g saturated fat, 11g protein,
47g carbs, 4g fiber, 25g sugar,
472mg sodium

Vanilla-Cherry-Almond Muffins

Sometimes muffins can be too sugary and heavy. Adding cherry-almond filling makes these muffins light and not too sweet. The cherries create very moist muffins which keep well for days, and the surprise of biting into a piece of fruit is always lovely. A favorite with kids and adults, these muffins are great for morning, afternoon, snack, or a picnic dessert!

1 pkg **Vanilla Cake & Baking Mix** (requires 2 eggs, ½ cup melted butter or ½ cup oil, and 1 cup cold milk)

1 cup jarred **Dark Morello Cherries**, drained and chopped

½ cup **Just Almond Meal**

Prep time 15 minutes
Hands-off cooking time 15-20 minutes
Makes 12 muffins

1 Preheat oven to 375°F.

2 Prepare cake batter as directed. Stir in cherries and almond meal. Mix well.

3 Lightly oil one 12-cup standard muffin pan or line with paper baking cups. Portion batter into muffin cups, ⅔ full.

4 Bake 15-20 minutes or until a toothpick inserted near center comes out clean. Let cool in pan on cooling rack 5-8 minutes. Remove muffins from pan. Cool completely.

Nutrition Snapshot
Per muffin: 280 calories, 12g fat, 6g saturated fat, 5g protein, 39g carbs, 1g fiber, 23g sugar, 34mg sodium

Homemade Healthy Cereal Bars

My husband is an avid mountain biker, and cereal bars are a must to avoid "bonking" when biking miles and miles. However, he was never able to find a bar he really liked. Despite so many cereal bar varieties available nowadays in stores, it's not easy to find a one that is not too sweet or too hard. One day I decided to make my own. The ingredient list here may be among the longest in this book, but these bars are both delicious and healthy!

2 cups **Praline Pecan Granola** or your favorite granola

5 **dried pitted apricots, chopped**

5 **pitted prunes, chopped**

5 **pitted dates, chopped**

1 **Tbsp flaxseed**

½ cup **Sesame Honey Almonds** or whole almonds, chopped

¼ cup **liquid honey**

1 **tsp vanilla extract**

Pinch salt

¼ cup **brown sugar**

¼ cup **creamy peanut butter**

Prep time 20 minutes
Hands-off cooking time 15-20 minutes
Makes 16 bars

  * Use gluten-free granola.

1 Preheat oven to 325°F.

2 Line bottom of a rimmed 7 x 11-inch baking sheet with parchment paper.

3 Combine granola, dried fruits, flaxseed, and almonds in medium bowl. Mix well.

4 Combine honey, vanilla, salt, brown sugar, and peanut butter in a large saucepan over medium-low heat, stirring well until all ingredients are blended together (do not bring to a boil). Remove pan from heat. Add granola mixture and stir to incorporate.

5 Spread mixture on prepared baking sheet. Cover with another sheet of parchment paper and press with your hands to create an even surface. Remove the top sheet of parchment paper.

6 Bake for 15-20 minutes until golden. Remove from oven and let cool for 5-10 minutes. Cut into squares or bars. If you see that the squares are a little fragile and not firm enough, let stand in the baking sheet a little longer before cutting.
Store in a tin or airtight container for up to one week.

Variation Substitute almond butter or other nut butter for peanut butter.

Nutrition Snapshot
Per bar: 147 calories, 5g fat, 1g saturated fat, 3g protein, 23g carbs, 2g fiber, 15g sugar, 40mg sodium

Greek Yogurt with Nuts and Honey

Greek yogurt is thicker and creamier than American yogurt, with a texture that is rich and velvety. Trader Joe's carries its own private-label brand at an attractive price. During a vacation in the Greek Islands, we discovered Greek yogurt topped with nuts, honey, and fresh fruits, served for breakfast. This snack is healthy and complete, simultaneously crunchy and silky. As a portable food, it is easy to pour and transport in a chilled container for breakfast, lunch, and snack.

1 cup plain Greek yogurt

1 Tbsp Pecan Praline Granola or your favorite granola

1 Tbsp golden raisins

1 Tbsp honey

1 Tbsp walnuts, chopped

Prep time 5 minutes
Serves 1

  * Use gluten-free granola

1 Spoon yogurt into a lidded container. Top with granola and raisins.

2 Drizzle with honey and sprinkle with nuts.

Variation
Add fresh fruit cut in small pieces.

Nutrition Snapshot
Per serving: 423 calories, 24g fat, 12g saturated fat, 11g protein, 43g carbs, 1g fiber, 32g sugar, 119mg sodium

Almond and Pear Brownie Muffins

Can you tell I'm fond of muffin recipes with fruit inside? Chocolate and pear are wonderful together, bringing rich flavor and moistness to this brownie treat. Brownies tend to crumble and smash when not properly packed. Baking brownies into muffin shapes makes them easier to carry and transport, preserving your precious dessert until it's time to enjoy it. Chocoholics will love the deep chocolate-truffle flavor and melt-in-your-mouth fudge-like texture. These muffins keep for 2-3 days in a tin.

2 pieces jarred **Pear Halves in White Grape Juice**
or 2 pieces jarred **Peach Halves in White Grape Juice**, drained

1 pkg **Truffle Brownie Mix** (prepared with 2 large eggs
and ½ cup melted butter)

1 cup **Just Almond Meal**

Prep time 15 minutes
Hands-off cooking time 20 minutes
Makes 12 muffins

1 Preheat oven to 350°F.

2 Cut pear halves into ½-inch pieces.

3 Prepare brownie batter according to package directions.
Add almond meal to brownie batter and mix well. Gently fold in pears.

4 Portion batter into a 12-cup standard muffin pan lined with paper baking cups.

5 Bake for 20 minutes. Let cool 30 minutes.

Nutrition Snapshot

*Per muffin: 276 calories, 14g fat, 5g saturated fat, 5g protein,
34g carbs, 3g fiber, 24g sugar, 99mg sodium*

Pearfectly Peachy Cherry Sauce

This sweet and tangy sauce has been a hit with my son. When my kids were little, I would make fresh fruit sauces because I did not like store-bought brands. It's also wonderful to experiment with fruit combinations beyond conventional (i.e., boring) applesauce. If I was caught without fresh fruits on hand, I would simply open a jar of peach or pear halves and purée it. Now, I'm in the habit of making a large batch of fruit sauce once a week, putting it into smaller containers for my kids' lunchboxes.

⅓ cup jarred **Dark Morello Cherries**, drained
2 pieces jarred **Pear Halves in White Grape Juice**, drained and chopped
2 pieces jarred **Peach Halves in White Grape Juice**, drained and chopped

Prep time 5 minutes
Serves 2

1 Put all ingredients in a food processor or a blender. Blend until smooth.

2 Place in a glass container, such as a large lidded jar, and chill. Keeps for 2-3 days.

Nutrition Snapshot
Per serving: 187 calories, 0g fat, 0g saturated fat, 1g protein, 44g carbs, 2g fiber, 33g sugar, 21mg sodium

Cherry Mini-Pies

These handheld fruit pies are easy to make, cute to look at, and not too sweet.
Fill them with any fruit sauce you like, or use the "Pearfectly Peachy Cherry Sauce" on p. 243.

1 frozen pie crust, thawed

½ cup jarred **Dark Morello Cherries**, drained and finely chopped

2 tsp sugar

1 tsp lemon juice

1 egg beaten with 1 tsp water for egg wash

Prep time 15 minutes
Hands-off cooking time 15-20 minutes
Makes 5 cherry pies

1 Preheat oven to 375°F.

2 On a lightly floured surface, roll out and stretch crust.
Cut out 10 (3-inch) circles with a round cutter or a drinking glass.

3 In a bowl, combine cherries, sugar and lemon juice. Toss to coat.

4 Mound cherry mixture in the centers of 5 crust circles, leaving a ½-inch edge.
Lightly brush edges with egg wash. Top each pie with another crust circle
and press edges firmly to seal. Using a fork, crimp edges.

5 Transfer pies to oiled or parchment-paper-lined baking sheet.
Brush pies with egg wash. Bake for 15-20 minutes until golden and puffed.

Nutrition Snapshot
Per mini-pie: 161 calories, 9g fat, 1g saturated fat, 2g protein,
20g carbs, 0g fiber, 5g sugar, 169mg sodium

Applesauce Mini-Pies

1 frozen pie crust, thawed

½ cup **Organic Unsweetened or Sweetened Applesauce**

1 egg beaten with 1 tsp water for egg wash

Prep time 15 minutes
Hands-off cooking time 15-20 minutes
Makes 5 apple pies

1 Preheat oven to 375°F.

2 On a lightly floured surface, roll out and stretch crust. Cut out 10 (3-inch) circles with a round cutter or a glass.

3 Mound applesauce in the centers of 5 crust circles, leaving a ½-inch edge. Lightly brush edges with egg wash. Top each pie with another crust circle and press edges firmly to seal. Using a fork, crimp edges.

4 Transfer pies to oiled or parchment-paper-lined baking sheet. Brush pies with egg wash. Bake for 15-20 minutes until golden and puffed.

Note

For the filling, you may mix cherries and apple sauce or pear sauce or use any other combination of your liking.

Nutrition Snapshot

Per mini-pie: 143 calories, 9g fat, 1g saturated fat, 1g protein, 15g carbs, 1g fiber, 2g sugar, 172mg sodium

Dried Fruit Compote

This compote is so simple and is a staple in France during the winter months. To make it, you need only dried fruits, juice, tea, honey and cinnamon. Instead of green or black tea, you could use chamomile (caffeine free) or any other herbal tea – ideal if you want to share this with your kids! Feel free to add any spices or cloves to enhance the festive and exotic taste. Delicious with ice cream or yogurt!

Freshly squeezed juice of 1 orange

1 cup water

1 Tbsp sugar

½ tsp ground cinnamon

1 bag green or black tea

3 dried apricots, pitted

4 prunes, pitted

3 dried Medjool Dates, pitted

1 tsp vanilla extract

1 tsp honey

Prep time 10 minutes
(not counting 35 minutes infusion time)
Serves 2

1   In a saucepan over medium–high heat, combine orange juice, water, sugar, and cinnamon. When boiling, add tea bag and let infuse for 5 minutes. Turn heat off and discard tea bag.

2   Add dried fruits and cover for at least 30 minutes. Heat again on medium heat and add vanilla. Cook for 5 minutes. Let cool and drizzle with honey.

Note

This marmalade is delicious with Greek yogurt or Homemade Almond Croissants (p. 233).

Nutrition Snapshot

Per serving: 224 calories, 0g fat, 224g saturated fat, 224g protein, 224g carbs, 224g fiber, 224g sugar, 224mg sodium

Chocolate Cocoa Pudding

1 cup semi-sweet chocolate chips
1 tsp unsweetened cocoa powder
2 cups whole milk
⅓ cup sugar
2 egg yolks
1 Tbsp corn starch

Prep time 20 minutes
Serves 4

1 In a medium saucepan over medium heat, combine chocolate chips, cocoa powder, milk, and sugar. Bring to a low boil, mixing well. As soon as mixture is smooth, remove from heat and set aside for 3 minutes to cool.

2 In a mixing bowl, mix eggs and corn starch. Add chocolate mixture a bit at a time, whisking well. Once combined, transfer this mixture back into saucepan. Cook over low heat and whisk without stopping for 2 minutes.

3 Pour pudding into 4 small ramekins or jars and set aside to cool. Cover with plastic wrap and place ramekins in fridge to rest for a few hours before eating.

Nutrition Snapshot *Per serving: 493 calories, 22g fat, 13g saturated fat, 9g protein, 64g carbs, 4g fiber, 55g sugar, 53mg sodium*

Petite Clafoutis

2 Tbsp all-purpose flour
2 large eggs
⅔ cup whole milk
⅓ cup plus 1 Tbsp sugar
1 ½ tsp vanilla extract
Pinch salt
1 cup jarred **Dark Morello Cherries**, drained

Prep time 10 minutes
Hands-off cooking time 20-25 minutes
Makes 4 clafoutis

1 Preheat oven to 400°F.

2 In a bowl, mix flour, eggs, milk, ⅓ cup sugar, vanilla extract, and salt just until custard is smooth.

3 Arrange cherries in one layer on buttered mini tartlet pans. Pour custard over cherries and bake for 20-25 minutes, or until top is puffed. Sprinkle with remaining sugar.

Nutrition Snapshot *Per clafouti: 207 calories, 4g fat, 1g saturated fat, 5g protein, 38g carbs, 1g fiber, 31g sugar, 91mg sodium*

Bread, Butter, and Chocolate

Le quatre-heure or goûter *(literally translated "the four o'clock") is the name for the afternoon snack ritual in France, and it is very serious business. Snacks are enjoyed around the kitchen table, and mothers often join their kids to talk about the day. Bread and butter are the base ingredients; additions may include milk chocolate bars, dark chocolate bars, jam, Gruyère cheese, powdered chocolate, or honey. Of course my choice was always dark chocolate, which on some days I would melt a little and spread thickly on bread. Oh trop bon!*

1 (3.5-oz) dark chocolate bar
¼ **Par Baked Baguette**, baked as instructed (or one very fresh, crispy baguette)
1 Tbsp unsalted butter, softened

Prep time 5 minutes
Serves 2

1 Break chocolate bar into small squares.

2 Slice baguette piece in two, lengthwise. Spread butter on each side, then trap chocolate squares between buttered baguette halves.

Nutrition Snapshot
Per serving: 454 calories, 31g fat, 19g saturated fat, 9g protein, 38g carbs, 9g fiber, 7g sugar, 151mg sodium

Choco-Crispy Rice Treats

Rice crispy treats are one of the most popular and nostalgic American treats. I created an all-natural version (not lacking any of the sweet deliciousness of the classic) that the whole family loves. Perfect for Christmas, Easter, or Valentine's day, I like to tuck these in my kids' lunchboxes as a special treat. These bite-size portions are pretty and portable. Alternatively, spread the mix on a baking sheet and cut into bars the traditional way!

9 oz semi-sweet chocolate chips

2 Tbsp unsalted butter

⅓ cup sugar

⅓ cup honey

3 cups **Crisp Rice** (rice crispies) cereal

Prep time 15 minutes

Hands-off cooking time 25-30 minutes

Makes 15 treats

1 In a saucepan over low heat, melt chocolate, butter, sugar, and honey. Mix well, and then add cereal.

2 Pour into small individual baking cups and refrigerate.

Nutrition Snapshot

Per treat: 243 calories, 10g fat, 6g saturated fat, 2g protein, 36g carbs, 2g fiber, 28g sugar, 50mg sodium

Almond Butter, Banana, and Honey Quesadillas

The flour tortilla is a staple ingredient in Southern California homes. This darling snack is a combination of almond butter and banana. Made in no time, you can experiment with different types of nut butters and a variety of fruits.

6 tsp **Almond Butter with Roasted Flaxseeds**

2 **flour tortillas**

½ **banana, thinly sliced**

2 tsp **honey**

Prep time 5 minutes
Hands-off cooking time 6-10 minutes
Serves 1

1 Spread almond butter on each tortilla, spreading from center to within an inch of the edge.

2 Arrange banana slices evenly on one tortilla.
   Drizzle with honey, then top with the other tortilla. Press gently.

3 On a lightly oiled griddle or skillet over medium heat, grill tortilla sandwich 3-5 minutes per side. Cut into wedges.

Nutrition Snapshot
Per serving: 481 calories, 22g fat, 3g saturated fat, 13g protein, 62g carbs, 7g fiber, 481g sugar, 481mg sodium

Index

Trader Joe's Store Locations

ARIZONA

Ahwatukee # 177
4025 E. Chandler Blvd.,
Ste. 38
Ahwatukee, AZ 85048
Phone: 480-759-2295

Glendale # 085
7720 West Bell Road
Glendale, AZ 85308
Phone: 623-776-7414

Mesa # 089
2050 East Baseline Rd.
Mesa, AZ 85204
Phone: 480-632-0951

Paradise Valley # 282
4726 E. Shea Blvd.
Phoenix, AZ 85028
Phone: 602-485-7788

**Phoenix
(Town & Country) # 090**
4821 N. 20th Street
Phoenix, AZ 85016
Phone: 602-912-9022

Scottsdale (North) # 087
7555 E. Frank Lloyd Wright
N. Scottsdale, AZ 85260
Phone: 480-367-8920

Scottsdale # 094
6202 N. Scottsdale Road
Scottsdale, AZ 85253
Phone: 480-948-9886

Surprise # 092
14095 West Grand Ave.
Surprise, AZ 85374
Phone: 623-546-1640

Tempe # 093
6460 S. McClintock Drive
Tempe, AZ 85283
Phone: 480-838-4142

**Tucson
(Crossroads) # 088**
4766 East Grant Road
Tucson, AZ 85712
Phone: 520-323-4500

**Tucson (Wilmot &
Speedway)# 095**
1101 N. Wilmot Rd.
Suite #147
Tucson, AZ 85712
Phone: 520-733-1313

**Tucson (Campbell &
Limberlost) # 191**
4209 N. Campbell Ave.
Tucson, AZ 85719
Phone: 520-325-0069

Tucson - Oro Valley # 096
7912 N. Oracle
Oro Valley, AZ 85704
Phone: 520-797-4207

CALIFORNIA

Agoura Hills
28941 Canwood Street
Agoura Hills, CA 91301
Phone: 818-865-8217

Alameda # 109
2217 South Shore Center
Alameda, CA 94501
Phone: 510-769-5450

Aliso Viejo # 195
The Commons
26541 Aliso Creek Road
Aliso Viejo, CA 92656
Phone: 949-643-5531

Arroyo Grande # 117
955 Rancho Parkway
Arroyo Grande, CA 93420
Phone: 805-474-6114

Bakersfield # 014
8200-C 21 Stockdale Hwy.
Bakersfield, CA 93311
Phone: 661-837-8863

Berkeley #186
1885 University Ave.
Berkeley, CA 94703
Phone: 510-204-9074

Bixby Knolls # 116
4121 Atlantic Ave.
Bixby Knolls, CA 90807
Phone: 562-988-0695

Brea # 011
2500 E. Imperial Hwy.
Suite 177
Brea, CA 92821
Phone 714-257-1180

Brentwood # 201
5451 Lone Tree Way
Brentwood, CA 94513
Phone: 925-516-3044

Burbank # 124
214 East Alameda
Burbank, CA 91502
Phone: 818-848-4299

Camarillo # 114
363 Carmen Drive
Camarillo, CA 93010
Phone: 805-388-1925

Campbell # 073
1875 Bascom Avenue
Campbell, CA 95008
Phone: 408-369-7823

Capitola # 064
3555 Clares Street #D
Capitola, CA 95010
Phone: 831-464-0115

Carlsbad # 220
2629 Gateway Road
Carlsbad, CA 92009
Phone: 760-603-8473

Castro Valley # 084
22224 Redwood Road
Castro Valley, CA 94546
Phone: 510-538-2738

Cathedral City # 118
67-720 East Palm Cyn.
Cathedral City, CA 92234
Phone: 760-202-0090

Cerritos # 104
12861 Towne Center Drive
Cerritos, CA 90703
Phone: 562-402-5148

Chatsworth # 184
10330 Mason Ave.
Chatsworth, CA 91311
Phone: 818-341-3010

Chico # 199
801 East Ave., Suite #110
Chico, CA 95926
Phone: 530-343-9920

Chino Hills # 216
13911 Peyton Dr.
Chino Hills, CA 91709
Phone: 909-627-1404

Chula Vista # 120
878 Eastlake Parkway,
Suite 810
Chula Vista, CA 91914
Phone: 619-656-5370

Claremont # 214
475 W. Foothill Blvd.
Claremont, CA 91711
Phone: 909-625-8784

Clovis # 180
1077 N. Willow, Suite 101
Clovis, CA 93611
Phone: 559-325-3120

**Concord (Oak Grove
& Treat) # 083**
785 Oak Grove Road
Concord, CA 94518
Phone: 925-521-1134

Concord (Airport) # 060
1150 Concord Ave.
Concord, CA 94520
Phone: 925-689-2990

Corona # 213
2790 Cabot Drive, Ste. 165
Corona, CA 92883
Phone: 951-603-0299

Costa Mesa # 035
640 W. 17th Street
Costa Mesa, CA 92627
Phone: 949-642-5134

Culver City # 036
9290 Culver Blvd.
Culver City, CA 90232
Phone: 310-202-1108

Daly City # 074
417 Westlake Center
Daly City, CA 94015
Phone: 650-755-3825

Danville # 065
85 Railroad Ave.
Danville, CA 94526
Phone: 925-838-5757

Davis
885 Russell Blvd.
Davis, CA 95616
Phone: 530-757-2693

Eagle Rock # 055
1566 Colorado Blvd.
Eagle Rock, CA 90041
Phone: 323-257-6422

El Cerrito # 108
225 El Cerrito Plaza
El Cerrito, CA 94530
Phone: 510-524-7609

Elk Grove # 190
9670 Bruceville Road
Elk Grove, CA 95757
Phone: 916-686-9980

Emeryville # 072
5700 Christie Avenue
Emeryville, CA 94608
Phone: 510-658-8091

Encinitas # 025
115 N. El Camino Real,
Suite A
Encinitas, CA 92024
Phone: 760-634-2114

Encino # 056
17640 Burbank Blvd.
Encino, CA 91316
Phone: 818-990-7751

Escondido # 105
1885 So. Centre City
Pkwy., Unit "A"
Escondido, CA 92025
Phone: 760-233-4020

Fair Oaks # 071
5309 Sunrise Blvd.
Fair Oaks, CA 95628
Phone: 916-863-1744

Fairfield # 101
1350 Gateway Blvd.,
Suite A1-A7
Fairfield, CA 94533
Phone: 707-434-0144

Folsom # 172
850 East Bidwell
Folsom, CA 95630
Phone: 916-817-8820

Fremont # 077
39324 Argonaut Way
Fremont, CA 94538
Phone: 510-794-1386

Fresno # 008
5376 N. Blackstone
Fresno, CA 93710
Phone: 559-222-4348

Glendale # 053
130 N. Glendale Ave.
Glendale, CA 91206
Phone: 818-637-2990

Goleta # 110
5767 Calle Real
Goleta, CA 93117
Phone: 805-692-2234

Granada Hills # 044
11114 Balboa Blvd.
Granada Hills, CA 91344
Phone: 818-368-6461

Hollywood
1600 N. Vine Street
Los Angeles, CA 90028
Phone: 323-856-0689

Huntington Bch. # 047
18681-101 Main Street
Huntington Bch., CA 92648
Phone: 714-848-9640

Huntington Bch. # 241
21431 Brookhurst St.
Huntington Bch., CA 92646
Phone: 714-968-4070

Huntington Harbor # 244
Huntington Harbour Mall
16821 Algonquin St.
Huntington Bch., CA 92649
Phone: 714-846-7307

Irvine (Walnut Village Center) # 037
14443 Culver Drive
Irvine, CA 92604
Phone: 949-857-8108

Irvine (University Center) # 111
4225 Campus Dr.
Irvine, CA 92612
Phone: 949-509-6138

Irvine (Irvine & Sand Cyn) # 210
6222 Irvine Blvd.
Irvine, CA 92620
Phone: 949-551-6402

La Cañada # 042
475 Foothill Blvd.
La Canada, CA 91011
Phone: 818-790-6373

La Crescenta # 052
3433 Foothill Blvd.
LaCrescenta, CA 91214
Phone: 818-249-3693

La Quinta # 189
46-400 Washington Street
La Quinta, CA 92253
Phone: 760-777-1553

Lafayette # 115
3649 Mt. Diablo Blvd.
Lafayette, CA 94549
Phone: 925-299-9344

Laguna Hills # 039
24321 Avenue De La
Carlota
Laguna Hills, CA 92653
Phone: 949-586-8453

Laguna Niguel # 103
32351 Street of the Golden
Lantern
Laguna Niguel, CA 92677
Phone: 949-493-8599

La Jolla # 020
8657 Villa LaJolla
Drive #210
La Jolla, CA 92037
Phone: 858-546-8629

La Mesa # 024
5495 Grossmont Center Dr.
La Mesa, CA 91942
Phone: 619-466-0105

Larkspur # 235
2052 Redwood Hwy
Larkspur, CA 94921
Phone: 415-945-7955

Livermore # 208
1122-A East Stanley Blvd.
Livermore, CA 94550
Phone: 925-243-1947

Long Beach (PCH) # 043
6451 E. Pacific Coast Hwy.
Long Beach, CA 90803
Phone: 562-596-4388

Long Beach (Bellflower Blvd.) # 194
2222 Bellflower Blvd.
Long Beach, CA 90815
Phone: 562-596-2514

Los Altos # 127
2310 Homestead Rd.
Los Altos, CA 94024
Phone: 408-245-1917

Los Angeles (Silver Lake) # 017
2738 Hyperion Ave.
Los Angeles, CA 90027
Phone: 323-665-6774

Los Angeles # 031
263 S. La Brea
Los Angeles, CA 90036
Phone: 323-965-1989

Los Angeles (Sunset Strip) # 192
8000 Sunset Blvd.
Los Angeles, CA 90046
Phone: 323-822-7663

Los Gatos # 181
15466 Los Gatos Blvd.
Los Gatos, CA 95032
Phone 408-356-2324

Manhattan Beach # 034
1821 Manhattan
Beach. Blvd.
Manhattan Bch., CA 90266
Phone: 310-372-1274

Manhattan Beach # 196
1800 Rosecrans Blvd.
Manhattan Beach,
CA 90266
Phone: 310-725-9800

Menlo Park # 069
720 Menlo Avenue
Menlo Park, CA 94025
Phone: 650-323-2134

Millbrae # 170
765 Broadway
Millbrae, CA 94030
Phone: 650-259-9142

Mission Viejo # 126
25410 Marguerite Parkway
Mission Viejo, CA 92692
Phone: 949-581-5638

Modesto # 009
3250 Dale Road
Modesto, CA 95356
Phone: 209-491-0445

Monrovia # 112
604 W. Huntington Dr.
Monrovia, CA 91016
Phone: 626-358-8884

Monterey # 204
570 Munras Ave., Ste. 20
Monterey, CA 93940
Phone: 831-372-2010

Morgan Hill # 202
17035 Laurel Road
Morgan Hill, CA 95037
Phone: 408-778-6409

Mountain View # 081
590 Showers Dr.
Mountain View, CA 94040
Phone: 650-917-1013

Napa # 128
3654 Bel Aire Plaza
Napa, CA 94558
Phone: 707-256-0806

Newbury Park # 243
125 N. Reino Road
Newbury Park, CA
Phone: 805-375-1984

Newport Beach # 125
8086 East Coast Highway
Newport Beach, CA 92657
Phone: 949-494-7404

Novato # 198
7514 Redwood Blvd.
Novato, CA 94945
Phone: 415-898-9359

**Oakland
(Lakeshore) # 203**
3250 Lakeshore Ave.
Oakland, CA 94610
Phone: 510-238-9076

**Oakland
(Rockridge) # 231**
5727 College Ave.
Oakland, CA 94618
Phone: 510-923-9428

Oceanside # 22
2570 Vista Way
Oceanside, CA 92054
Phone: 760-433-9994

Orange # 046
2114 N. Tustin St.
Orange, CA 92865
Phone: 714-283-5697

Pacific Grove # 008
1170 Forest Avenue
Pacific Grove, CA 93950
Phone: 831-656-0180

Palm Desert # 003
44-250 Town Center Way,
Suite C6
Palm Desert, CA 92260
Phone: 760-340-2291

Palmdale # 185
39507 10th Street West
Palmdale, CA 93551
Phone: 661-947-2890

Palo Alto # 207
855 El Camino Real
Palo Alto, CA 94301
Phone: 650-327-7018

**Pasadena
(S. Lake Ave.) # 179**
345 South Lake Ave.
Pasadena, CA 91101
Phone: 626-395-9553

**Pasadena
(S. Arroyo Pkwy.) # 051**
610 S. Arroyo Parkway
Pasadena, CA 91105
Phone: 626-568-9254

**Pasadena
(Hastings Ranch) # 171**
467 Rosemead Blvd.
Pasadena, CA 91107
Phone: 626-351-3399

Petaluma # 107
169 North McDowell Blvd.
Petaluma, CA 94954
Phone: 707-769-2782

Pinole # 230
2742 Pinole Valley Rd.
Pinole, CA 94564
Phone: 510-222-3501

Pleasanton # 066
4040 Pimlico #150
Pleasanton, CA 94588
Phone: 925-225-3600

Rancho Cucamonga # 217
6401 Haven Ave.
Rancho Cucamonga, CA
91737
Phone: 909-476-1410

**Rancho Palos Verdes
057**
28901 S. Western Ave. #243
Rancho Palos Verdes,
CA 90275
Phone: 310-832-1241

**Rancho Palos Verdes
233**
31176 Hawthorne Blvd.
Rancho Palos Verdes,
CA 90275
Phone: 310-544-1727

**Rancho Santa
Margarita # 027**
30652 Santa Margarita
Pkwy. Suite F102
Rancho Santa Margarita,
CA 92688
Phone: 949-888-3640

Redding # 219
845 Browning St.
Redding, CA 96003
Phone: 530-223-4875

Redlands # 099
552 Orange Street Plaza
Redlands, CA 92374
Phone: 909-798-3888

Redondo Beach # 038
1761 S. Elena Avenue
Redondo Bch., CA 90277
Phone: 310-316-1745

Riverside # 15
6225 Riverside Plaza
Riverside, CA 92506
Phone: 951-682-4684

Roseville # 80
1117 Roseville Square
Roseville, CA 95678
Phone: 916-784-9084

**Sacramento
(Folsom Blvd.) # 175**
5000 Folsom Blvd.
Sacramento, CA 95819
Phone: 916-456-1853

**Sacramento
(Fulton & Marconi) # 070**
2625 Marconi Avenue
Sacramento, CA 95821
Phone: 916-481-8797

San Carlos # 174
1482 El Camino Real
San Carlos, CA 94070
Phone: 650-594-2138

San Clemente # 016
638 Camino DeLosMares,
Sp.#115-G
San Clemente, CA 92673
Phone: 949-240-9996

**San Diego
(Hillcrest) # 026**
1090 University Ste.
G100-107
San Diego, CA 92103
Phone: 619-296-3122

**San Diego
(Point Loma) # 188**
2401 Truxtun Rd., Ste. 300
San Diego, CA 92106
Phone: 619-758-9272

**San Diego
(Pacific Beach) # 021**
1211 Garnet Avenue
San Diego, CA 92109
Phone: 858-272-7235

**San Diego (Carmel Mtn.
Ranch) # 023**
11955 Carmel Mtn. Rd.
#702
San Diego, CA 92128
Phone: 858-673-0526

**San Diego
(Scripps Ranch) # 221**
9850 Hibert Street
San Diego, CA 92131
Phone: 858-549-9185

San Dimas # 028
856 Arrow Hwy. "C"
Target Center
San Dimas, CA 91773
Phone: 909-305-4757

**San Francisco
(9th Street) # 078**
555 9th Street
San Francisco, CA 94103
Phone: 415-863-1292

**San Francisco
(Masonic Ave.) # 100**
3 Masonic Avenue
San Francisco, CA 94118
Phone: 415-346-9964

**San Francisco
(North Beach) # 019**
401 Bay Street
San Francisco, CA 94133
Phone: 415-351-1013

**San Francisco
(Stonestown) # 236**
265 Winston Dr.
San Francisco, CA 94132
Phone: 415-665-1835

San Gabriel # 032
7260 N. Rosemead Blvd.
San Gabriel, CA 91775
Phone: 626-285-5862

San Jose (Bollinger) # 232
7250 Bollinger Rd.
San Jose, CA 95129
Phone: 408-873-7384

**San Jose
(Coleman Ave) # 212**
635 Coleman Ave.
San Jose, CA 95110
Phone: 408-298-9731

**San Jose
(Old Almaden) # 063**
5353 Almaden Expressway
#J-38
San Jose, CA 95118
Phone: 408-927-9091

**San Jose
(Westgate West) # 062**
5269 Prospect
San Jose, CA 95129
Phone: 408-446-5055

San Luis Obispo # 041
3977 Higuera Street
San Luis Obispo, CA 93401
Phone: 805-783-2780

**San Mateo
(Grant Street) # 067**
1820-22 S. Grant Street
San Mateo, CA 94402
Phone: 650-570-6140

**San Mateo
(Hillsdale) # 245**
45 W Hillsdale Blvd
San Mateo, CA 94403
Phone: 650-286-1509

San Rafael # 061
337 Third Street
San Rafael, CA 94901
Phone: 415-454-9530

Santa Ana # 113
3329 South Bristol Street
Santa Ana, CA 92704
Phone: 714-424-9304

**Santa Barbara
(S. Milpas St.) # 059**
29 S. Milpas Street
Santa Barbara, CA 93103
Phone: 805-564-7878

**Santa Barbara
(De La Vina) # 183**
3025 De La Vina
Santa Barbara, CA 93105
Phone: 805-563-7383

Santa Cruz # 193
700 Front Street
Santa Cruz, CA 95060
Phone: 831-425-0140

Santa Maria # 239
1303 S. Bradley Road
Santa Maria, CA 93454
Phone: 805-925-1657

Santa Monica # 006
3212 Pico Blvd.
Santa Monica, CA 90405
Phone: 310-581-0253

**Santa Rosa
(Cleveland Ave.) # 075**
3225 Cleveland Avenue
Santa Rosa, CA 95403
Phone: 707-525-1406

**Santa Rosa
(Santa Rosa Ave.) # 178**
2100 Santa Rosa Ave.
Santa Rosa, CA 95407
Phone: 707-535-0788

Sherman Oaks # 049
14119 Riverside Drive
Sherman Oaks, CA 91423
Phone: 818-789-2771

Simi Valley # 030
2975-A Cochran St.
Simi Valley, CA 93065
Phone: 805-520-3135

South Pasadena # 018
613 Mission Street
South Pasadena, CA 91030
Phone: 626-441-6263

**South San Francisco
187**
301 McLellan Dr.
So. San Francisco,
CA 94080
Phone: 650-583-6401

Stockton # 076
6535 Pacific Avenue
Stockton, CA 95207
Phone: 209-951-7597

Studio City # 122
11976 Ventura Blvd.
Studio City, CA 91604
Phone: 818-509-0168

Sunnyvale # 068
727 Sunnyvale/
Saratoga Rd.
Sunnyvale, CA 94087
Phone: 408-481-9082

Temecula # 102
40665 Winchester Rd.,
Bldg. B, Ste. 4-6
Temecula, CA 92591
Phone: 951-296-9964

Templeton # 211
1111 Rossi Road
Templeton, CA 93465
Phone: 805-434-9562

Thousand Oaks # 196
451 Avenida
De Los Arboles
Thousand Oaks, CA 91360
Phone: 805-492-7107

Toluca Lake # 054
10130 Riverside Drive
Toluca Lake, CA 91602
Phone: 818-762-2787

**Torrance
(Hawthorne Blvd.) # 121**
19720 Hawthorne Blvd.
Torrance, CA 90503
Phone: 310-793-8585

**Torrance (Rolling
Hills Plaza) # 029**
2545 Pacific Coast Highway
Torrance, CA 90505
Phone: 310-326-9520

Tustin # 197
12932 Newport Avenue
Tustin, CA 92780
Phone: 714-669-3752

Upland # 010
333 So. Mountain Avenue
Upland, CA 91786
Phone: 909-946-4799

Valencia # 013
26517 Bouquet Canyon Rd
Santa Clarita, CA 91350
Phone: 661-263-3796

Ventura # 045
1795 S. Victoria Avenue
Ventura, CA 93003
Phone: 805-650-9977

Ventura – Midtown
103 S. Mills Road Suite 104
Ventura, CA 93003
Phone: 805-658-2664

Walnut Creek # 123
1372 So. California Blvd.
Walnut Creek, CA 94596
Phone: 925-945-1674

West Hills # 050
6751 Fallbrook Ave.
West Hills, CA 91307
Phone: 818-347-2591

West Hollywood # 040
7304 Santa Monica Blvd.
West Hollywood, CA 90046
Phone: 323-851-9772

West Hollywood # 173
8611 Santa Monica Blvd.
West Hollywood, CA 90069
Phone: 310-657-0152

**West Los Angeles
(National Blvd.) # 007**
10850 National Blvd.
West Los Angeles, CA
90064
Phone: 310-470-1917

**West Los Angeles
S. Sepulveda Blvd.) # 119**
3456 S. Sepulveda Blvd.
West Los Angeles,
CA 90034
Phone: 310-836-2458

**West Los Angeles
(Olympic) # 215**
11755 W. Olympic Blvd.
West Los Angeles,
CA 90064
Phone: 310-477-5949

Westchester # 033
8645 S. Sepulveda
Westchester, CA 90045
Phone: 310-338-9238

Westlake Village # 058
3835 E. Thousand
Oaks Blvd.
Westlake Village, CA 91362
Phone: 805-494-5040

Westwood # 234
1000 Glendon Avenue
Los Angeles, CA 90024
Phone: 310-824-1495

Whittier # 048
15025 E. Whittier Blvd.
Whittier, CA 90603
Phone: 562-698-1642

Woodland Hills # 209
21054 Clarendon St.
Woodland Hills, CA 91364
Phone: 818-712-9475

Yorba Linda # 176
19655 Yorba Linda Blvd.
Yorba Linda, CA 92886
Phone: 714-970-0116

CONNECTICUT
Danbury # 525
113 Mill Plain Rd.
Danbury, CT 06811
Phone: 203-739-0098
Alcohol: Beer Only

Darien # 522
436 Boston Post Rd.
Darien, CT 06820
Phone: 203-656-1414
Alcohol: Beer Only

Fairfield # 523
2258 Black Rock Turnpike
Fairfield, CT 06825
Phone: 203-330-8301
Alcohol: Beer Only

Orange # 524
560 Boston Post Road
Orange, CT 06477
Phone: 203-795-5505
Alcohol: Beer Only

West Hartford # 526
1489 New Britain Ave.
West Hartford, CT 06110
Phone: 860-561-4771
Alcohol: Beer Only

Westport # 521
400 Post Road East
Westport, CT 06880
Phone: 203-226-8966
Alcohol: Beer Only

DELAWARE
Wilmington* # 536
5605 Concord Pike
Wilmington, DE 19803
Phone: 302-478-8494

DISTRICT OF COLUMBIA
Washington # 653
1101 25th Street NW
Washington, DC 20037
Phone: 202-296-1921

GEORGIA

Athens
1850 Epps Bridge Parkway
Athens, GA 30606
Phone: 706-583-8934

**Atlanta
(Buckhead) # 735**
3183 Peachtree Rd NE
Atlanta, GA 30305
Phone: 404-842-0907

Atlanta (Midtown) # 730
931 Monroe Dr., NE
Atlanta, GA 30308
Phone: 404-815-9210

Marietta # 732
4250 Roswell Road
Marietta, GA 30062
Phone: 678-560-3585

Norcross # 734
5185 Peachtree Parkway,
Bld. 1200
Norcross, GA 30092
Phone: 678-966-9236

Roswell # 733
635 W. Crossville Road
Roswell, GA 30075
Phone: 770-645-8505

Sandy Springs # 731
6277 Roswell Road NE
Sandy Springs, GA 30328
Phone: 404-236-2414

ILLINOIS

Algonquin # 699
1800 South Randall Road
Algonquin, IL 60102
Phone: 847-854-4886

Arlington Heights # 687
17 W. Rand Road
Arlington Heights, IL 60004
Phone: 847-506-0752

Batavia # 689
1942 West Fabyan
Parkway #222
Batavia, IL 60510
Phone: 630-879-3234

**Chicago
River North) # 696**
44 E. Ontario St.
Chicago, IL 60611
Phone: 312-951-6369

**Chicago
(Lincoln & Grace) # 688**
3745 North Lincoln Avenue
Chicago, IL 60613
Phone: 773-248-4920

**Chicago
(Lincoln Park) # 691**
1840 North Clybourn
Avenue #200
Chicago, IL 60614
Phone: 312-274-9733

***Chicago (South Loop) –
coming soon!***
1147 S. Wabash Ave.
Chicago, IL 60605
Phone: TBD

***Chicago (Lakeview) –
coming soon!***
667 W. Diversey Pkwy
Chicago, IL 60614
Phone: 773-935-7255

Downers Grove # 683
122 Ogden Ave.
Downers Grove, IL 60515
Phone: 630-241-1662

Glen Ellyn # 680
680 Roosevelt Rd.
Glen Ellyn, IL 60137
Phone: 630-858-5077

Glenview # 681
1407 Waukegan Road
Glenview, IL 60025
Phone: 847-657-7821

La Grange # 685
25 North La Grange Road
La Grange, IL 60525
Phone: 708-579-0838

Lake Zurich # 684
735 W. Route 22**
Lake Zurich, IL 60047
Phone: 847-550-7827
[**For accurate driving
directions using
GPS, please use 735 W
Main Street]

Naperville # 690
44 West Gartner Road
Naperville, IL 60540
Phone: 630-355-4389

Northbrook # 682
127 Skokie Blvd.
Northbrook, IL 60062
Phone: 847-498-9076

Oak Park # 697
483 N. Harlem Ave.
Oak Park, IL 60301
Phone: 708-386-1169

Orland Park # 686
14924 S. La Grange Road
Orland Park, IL 60462
Phone: 708-349-9021

Park Ridge # 698
190 North Northwest
Highway
Park Ridge, IL 60068
Phone: 847-292-1108

INDIANA

**Indianapolis
(Castleton) # 671**
5473 East 82nd Street
Indianapolis, IN 46250
Phone: 317-595-8950

**Indianapolis
(West 86th) # 670**
2902 West 86th Street
Indianapolis, IN 46268
Phone: 317-337-1880

IOWA

West Des Moines
6305 Mills Civic Parkway
West Des Moines, IA 50266
Phone: 515-225-3820

KANSAS – Coming soon!

Leawood – coming soon!
4201 W 119th Street
Leawood, KS 66209
Phone: TBD

MAINE

Portland
87 Marginal Way
Portland, ME 04101
Phone: 207-699-3799

MARYLAND

Annapolis* # 650
160 F Jennifer Road
Annapolis, MD 21401
Phone: 410-573-0505

Bethesda* # 645
6831 Wisconsin Avenue
Bethesda, MD 20815
Phone: 301-907-0982

Columbia* # 658
6610 Marie Curie Dr. (Int.
of 175 & 108)
Elkridge, MD 21075
Phone: 410-953-8139

Gaithersburg* # 648
18270 Contour Rd.
Gaithersburg, MD 20877
Phone: 301-947-5953

Pikesville* # 655
1809 Reisterstown Road,
Suite #121
Pikesville, MD 21208
Phone: 410-484-8373

Rockville* # 642
12268-H Rockville Pike
Rockville, MD 20852
Phone: 301-468-6656

Silver Spring* # 652
10741 Columbia Pike
Silver Spring, MD 20901
Phone: 301-681-1675

Towson* # 649
1 E. Joppa Rd.
Towson, MD 21286
Phone: 410-296-9851

MASSACHUSETTS

Acton* # 511
145 Great Road
Acton, MA 01720
Phone: 978-266-8908

Arlington* # 505
1427 Massachusetts Ave.
Arlington, MA 02476
Phone: 781-646-9138

Boston #510
899 Boylston Street
Boston, MA 02115
Phone: 617-262-6505

Brookline # 501
1317 Beacon Street
Brookline, MA 02446
Phone: 617-278-9997

Burlington* # 515
51 Middlesex Turnpike
Burlington, MA 01803
Phone: 781-273-2310

Cambridge
748 Memorial Drive
Cambridge, MA 02139
Phone: 617-491-8582

**Cambridge
(Fresh Pond)* # 517**
211 Alewife Brook Pkwy
Cambridge, MA 02138
Phone: 617-498-3201

Framingham # 503
659 Worcester Road
Framingham, MA 01701
Phone: 508-935-2931

Hadley* # 512
375 Russell Street
Hadley, MA 01035
Phone: 413-587-3260

Hanover* # 513
1775 Washington Street
Hanover, MA 02339
Phone: 781-826-5389

Hyannis* # 514
Christmas Tree Promenade
655 Route 132, Unit 4-A
Hyannis, MA 02601
Phone: 508-790-3008

Needham Hts* 504
958 Highland Avenue
Needham Hts, MA 02494
Phone: 781-449-6993

Peabody* # 516
300 Andover Street,
Suite 15
Peabody, MA 01960
Phone: 978-977-5316

Saugus* # 506
358 Broadway, Unit B
(Shops @ Saugus, Rte. 1)
Saugus, MA 01906
Phone: 781-231-0369

Shrewsbury* # 508
77 Boston Turnpike
Shrewsbury, MA 01545
Phone: 508-755-9560

Tyngsboro* # 507
440 Middlesex Road
Tyngsboro, MA 01879
Phone: 978-649-2726

West Newton* # 509
1121 Washington St.
West Newton, MA 02465
Phone: 617-244-1620

MICHIGAN
Ann Arbor # 678
2398 East Stadium Blvd.
Ann Arbor, MI 48104
Phone: 734-975-2455

Farmington Hills # 675
31221 West 14 Mile Road
Farmington Hills, MI 48334
Phone: 248-737-4609

Grosse Pointe # 665
17028 Kercheval Ave.
Grosse Pointe, MI 48230
Phone: 313-640-7794

Northville # 667
20490 Haggerty Road
Northville, MI 48167
Phone: 734-464-3675

Rochester Hills # 668
3044 Walton Blvd.
Rochester Hills, MI 48309
Phone: 248-375-2190

Royal Oak # 674
27880 Woodward Ave.
Royal Oak, MI 48067
Phone: 248-582-9002

MINNESOTA
Maple Grove # 713
12105 Elm Creek Blvd. N.
Maple Grove, MN 55369
Phone: 763-315-1739

Minnetonka # 714
11220 Wayzata Blvd
Minnetonka, MN 55305
Phone: 952-417-9080

Rochester
1200 16th St. SW
Rochester, NY 55902
Phone: 952-417-9080

St. Louis Park # 710
4500 Excelsior Blvd.
St. Louis Park, MN 55416
Phone: 952-285-1053

St. Paul # 716
484 Lexington Parkway S.
St. Paul, MN 55116
Phone: 651-698-3119

Woodbury # 715
8960 Hudson Road
Woodbury, MN 55125
Phone: 651-735-0269

MISSOURI
Brentwood # 792
48 Brentwood
Promenade Court
Brentwood, MO 63144
Phone: 314-963-0253

Chesterfield # 693
1679 Clarkson Road
Chesterfield, MO 63017
Phone: 636-536-7846

Creve Coeur # 694
11505 Olive Blvd.
Creve Coeur, MO 63141
Phone: 314-569-0427

Des Peres # 695
13343 Manchester Rd.
Des Peres, MO 63131
Phone: 314-984-5051

*Kansas City –
coming soon!*
8600 Ward Parkway
Kansas City, MO 64114
Phone: TBD

NEBRASKA
Lincoln
3120 Pine Lake Road,
Suite R
Lincoln, NE 68516
Phone: 402-328-0120

Omaha # 714
10305 Pacific St.
Omaha, NE 68114
Phone: 402-391-3698

NEVADA
Anthem # 280
10345 South Eastern Ave.
Henderson, NV 89052
Phone: 702-407-8673

Carson City # 281
3790 US Highway 395 S,
Suite 401
Carson City, NV 89705
Phone: 775-267-2486

Henderson # 097
2716 North Green Valley
Parkway
Henderson, NV 89014
Phone: 702-433-6773

**Las Vegas
(Decatur Blvd.) # 098**
2101 S. Decatur Blvd.,
Suite 25
Las Vegas, NV 89102
Phone: 702-367-0227

**Las Vegas
(Summerlin) # 086**
7575 West Washington,
Suite 117
Las Vegas, NV 89128
Phone: 702-242-8240

Reno # 082
5035 S. McCarran Blvd.
Reno, NV 89502
Phone: 775-826-1621

NEW JERSEY
Edgewater* # 606
715 River Road
Edgewater, NJ 07020
Phone: 201-945-5932

Florham Park* # 604
186 Columbia Turnpike
Florham Park, NJ 07932
Phone: 973-514-1511

Marlton* # 631
300 P Route 73 South
Marlton, NJ 08053
Phone: 856-988-3323

Millburn* # 609
187 Millburn Ave.
Millburn, NJ 07041
Phone: 973-218-0912

Paramus* # 605
404 Rt. 17 North
Paramus, NJ 07652
Phone: 201-265-9624

Princeton # 607
3528 US 1
(Brunswick Pike)
Princeton, NJ 08540
Phone: 609-897-0581

Shrewsbury*
1031 Broad St.
Shrewsbury, NJ 07702
Phone: 732-389-2535

Wayne* # 632
1172 Hamburg Turnpike
Wayne, NJ 07470
Phone: 973-692-0050

Westfield # 601
155 Elm St.
Westfield, NJ 07090
Phone: 908-301-0910

Westwood* # 602
20 Irvington Street
Westwood, NJ 07675
Phone: 201-263-0134

NEW MEXICO
Albuquerque # 166
8928 Holly Ave. NE
Albuquerque, NM 87122
Phone: 505-796-0311

**Albuquerque
(Uptown) # 167**
2200 Uptown Loop NE
Albuquerque, NM 87110
Phone: 505-883-3662

Santa Fe # 165
530 W. Cordova Road
Santa Fe, NM 87505
Phone: 505-995-8145

NEW YORK
Brooklyn # 558
130 Court St
Brooklyn, NY 11201
Phone: 718-246-8460
Alcohol: Beer Only

Commack # 551
5010 Jericho Turnpike
Commack, NY 11725
Phone: 631-493-9210
Alcohol: Beer Only

Hartsdale # 533
215 North Central Avenue
Hartsdale, NY 10530
Phone: 914-997-1960
Alcohol: Beer Only

Hewlett # 554
1280 West Broadway
Hewlett, NY 11557
Phone: 516-569-7191
Alcohol: Beer Only

Lake Grove # 556
137 Alexander Ave.
Lake Grove, NY 11755
Phone: 631-863-2477
Alcohol: Beer Only

Larchmont # 532
1260 Boston Post Road
Larchmont, NY 10538
Phone: 914-833-9110
Alcohol: Beer Only

Merrick # 553
1714 Merrick Road
Merrick, NY 11566
Phone: 516-771-1012
Alcohol: Beer Only

**New York
(72nd & Broadway) # 542**
2075 Broadway
New York, NY 10023
Phone: 212-799-0028
Alcohol: Beer Only

**New York
(Chelsea) # 543**
675 6th Ave
New York, NY 10010
Phone: 212-255-2106
Alcohol: Beer Only

**New York (Union Square
Grocery) # 540**
142 E. 14th St.
New York, NY 10003
Phone: 212-529-4612
Alcohol: Beer Only

**New York (Union Square
Wine) # 541**
138 E. 14th St.
New York, NY 10003
Phone: 212-529-6326
Alcohol: Wine Only

Oceanside # 552
3418 Long Beach Rd.
Oceanside, NY 11572
Phone: 516-536-9163
Alcohol: Beer Only

Plainview # 555
425 S. Oyster Bay Rd.
Plainview, NY 11803
Phone: 516-933-6900
Alcohol: Beer Only

Queens # 557
90-30 Metropolitan Ave.
Queens, NY 11374
Phone: 718-275-1791
Alcohol: Beer Only

Scarsdale # 531
727 White Plains Rd.
Scarsdale, NY 10583
Phone: 914-472-2988
Alcohol: Beer Only

*Staten Island
– coming soon!*
2385 Richmond Ave
Staten Island, NY 10314
Phone: TBD
Alcohol: Beer Only

NORTH CAROLINA
Cary # 741
1393 Kildaire Farms Rd.
Cary, NC 27511
Phone: 919-465-5984

Chapel Hill # 745
1800 E. Franklin St.
Chapel Hill, NC 27514
Phone: 919-918-7871

**Charlotte
(Midtown) # 744**
1133 Metropolitan Ave.,
Ste. 100
Charlotte, NC 28204
Phone: 704-334-0737

Charlotte (North) # 743
1820 East Arbors Dr.**
(corner of W. Mallard Creek
Church Rd. & Senator
Royall Dr.)
Charlotte, NC 28262
Phone: 704-688-9578
[**For accurate driving di-
rections on the web, please
use 1820 W. Mallard Creek
Church Rd.]

Charlotte (South) # 742
6418 Rea Rd.
Charlotte, NC 28277
Phone: 704-543-5249

Raleigh # 746
3000 Wake Forest Rd.
Raleigh, NC 27609
Phone: 919-981-7422

OHIO
Cincinnati # 669
7788 Montgomery Road
Cincinnati, OH 45236
Phone: 513-984-3452

Columbus # 679
3888 Townsfair Way
Columbus, OH 43219
Phone: 614-473-0794

Dublin # 672
6355 Sawmill Road
Dublin, OH 43017
Phone: 614-793-8505

Kettering # 673
328 East Stroop Road
Kettering, OH 45429
Phone: 937-294-5411

Westlake # 677
175 Market Street
Westlake, OH 44145
Phone: 440-250-1592

Woodmere # 676
28809 Chagrin Blvd.
Woodmere, OH 44122
Phone: 216-360-9320

OREGON
Beaverton # 141
11753 S. W. Beaverton
Hillsdale Hwy.
Beaverton, OR 97005
Phone: 503-626-3794

Bend # 150
63455 North
Highway 97, Ste. 4
Bend, OR 97701
Phone: 541-312-4198

Clackamas # 152
9345 SE 82nd Ave (across
from Home Depot)
Happy Valley, OR 97086
Phone: 503-771-6300

Corvallis # 154
1550 NW 9th Street
Corvallis, OR 97330
Phone: 541-753-0048

Eugene # 145
85 Oakway Center
Eugene, OR 97401
Phone: 541-485-1744

Hillsboro # 149
2285 NW 185th Ave.
Hillsboro, OR 97124
Phone: 503-645-8321

Lake Oswego # 142
15391 S. W. Bangy Rd.
Lake Oswego, OR 97035
Phone: 503-639-3238

Portland (SE) # 143
4715 S. E. 39th Avenue
Portland, OR 97202
Phone: 503-777-1601

Portland (NW) # 146
2122 N.W. Glisan
Portland, OR 97210
Phone: 971-544-0788

**Portland
(Hollywood) # 144**
4121 N.E. Halsey St.
Portland, OR 97213
Phone: 503-284-1694

Salem – coming soon!
4450 Commercial St.,
Suite 100
Salem, OR 97302
Phone: TBD

PENNSYLVANIA
Ardmore* # 635
112 Coulter Avenue
Ardmore, PA 19003
Phone: 610-658-0645

Jenkintown* # 633
933 Old York Road
Jenkintown, PA 19046
Phone: 215-885-524

Media* # 637
12 East State Street
Media, PA 19063
Phone: 610-891-2752

North Wales* # 639
1430 Bethlehem Pike
(corner SR 309 & SR 63)
North Wales, PA 19454
Phone: 215-646-5870

Philadelphia* # 634
2121 Market Street
Philadelphia, PA 19103
Phone: 215-569-9282

Pittsburgh* # 638
6343 Penn Ave.
Pittsburgh, PA 15206
Phone: 412-363-5748

Pittsburgh
- coming soon!
1600 Washington Road
Pittsburgh, PA 15228
Phone: TBD

Wayne* # 632
171 East Swedesford Rd.
Wayne, PA 19087
Phone: 610-225-0925

RHODE ISLAND
Warwick* # 518
1000 Bald Hill Rd
Warwick, RI 02886
Phone: 401-821-5368

SOUTH CAROLINA
Greenville
59 Woodruff
Industrial Lane
Greenville, SC 29607
Phone: 864-286-0231

Mt. Pleasant –
coming soon!
401 Johnnie Dodds Blvd.
Mt. Pleasant, SC 29464
Phone: TBD

TENNESSEE
Nashville # 664
3909 Hillsboro Pike
Nashville, TN 37215
Phone: 615-297-6560
Alcohol: Beer Only

VIRGINIA
Alexandria # 647
612 N. Saint Asaph Street
Alexandria, VA 22314
Phone: 703-548-0611

Bailey's Crossroads # 644
5847 Leesburg Pike
Bailey's Crossroads,
VA 22041
Phone: 703-379-5883

Centreville # 654
14100 Lee Highway
Centreville, VA 20120
Phone: 703-815-0697

Fairfax # 643
9464 Main Street
Fairfax, VA 22031
Phone: 703-764-8550

Falls Church # 641
7514 Leesburg Turnpike
Falls Church, VA 22043
Phone: 703-288-0566

Newport News # 656
12551 Jefferson Ave.,
Suite #179
Newport News, VA 23602
Phone: 757-890-0235

Reston # 646
11958 Killingsworth Ave.
Reston, VA 20194
Phone: 703-689-0865

**Richmond
(Short Pump) # 659**
11331 W Broad St, Ste 161
Glen Allen, VA 23060
Phone: 804-360-4098

Springfield # 651
6394 Springfield Plaza
Springfield, VA 22150
Phone: 703-569-9301

Virginia Beach # 660
503 Hilltop Plaza
Virginia Beach, VA 23454
Phone: 757-422-4840

Williamsburg # 657
5000 Settlers Market Blvd
(corner of
Monticello and Settlers
Market)**
Williamsburg, VA 23188
Phone: 757-259-2135
[**For accurate driving di-
rections on the web, please
use 5224 Monticello Ave.]

WASHINGTON
Ballard # 147
4609 14th Avenue NW
Seattle, WA 98107
Phone: 206-783-0498

Bellevue # 131
15400 N. E. 20th Street
Bellevue, WA 98007
Phone: 425-643-6885

Bellingham # 151
2410 James Street
Bellingham, WA 98225
Phone: 360-734-5166

Burien # 133
15868 1st. Avenue South
Burien, WA 98148
Phone: 206-901-9339

Everett # 139
811 S.E. Everett Mall Way
Everett, WA 98208
Phone: 425-513-2210

Federal Way # 134
1758 S. 320th Street
Federal Way, WA 98003
Phone: 253-529-9242

Issaquah # 138
1495 11th Ave. N.W.
Issaquah, WA 98027
Phone: 425-837-8088

Kirkland # 132
12632 120th Avenue N. E.
Kirkland, WA 98034
Phone: 425-823-1685

Lynnwood # 129
19500 Highway 99,
Suite 100
Lynnwood, WA 98036
Phone: 425-744-1346

Olympia # 156
Olympia West Center
1530 Black Lake Blvd.
Olympia, WA 98502
Phone: 360-352-7440

Redmond # 140
15932 Redmond Way
Redmond, WA 98052
Phone: 425-883-1624

Seattle (U. District) # 137
4555 Roosevelt Way NE
Seattle, WA 98105
Phone: 206-547-6299

**Seattle
(Queen Anne Hill) # 135**
112 West Galer St.
Seattle, WA 98119
Phone: 206-378-5536

**Seattle
(Capitol Hill) # 130**
1700 Madison St.
Seattle, WA 98122
Phone: 206-322-7268

Spokane – coming soon!
2975 East 29th Avenue
Spokane, WA 99223
Phone: TBD

University Place # 148
3800 Bridgeport Way West
University Place, WA 98466
Phone: 253-460-2672

Vancouver # 136
305 SE Chkalov Drive #B1
Vancouver, WA 98683
Phone: 360-883-9000

WISCONSIN
Glendale # 711
5600 North Port
Washington Road
Glendale, WI 53217
Phone: 414-962-3382

Madison # 712
1810 Monroe Street
Madison, WI 53711
Phone: 608-257-1916

Notes

Photo Credits

All photos of recipes, outlined food images on pages 8, 18, 20, 32, 40, 92, 220 © Tia Black

By **shutterstock.com**, photos of fruits, vegetables, retro clip art, etc.on pages:
8, 9, 24, 30, 213, 219, 224, 229, 243, 254, 257, 261 © Andrjuss
183 © Eric Gevaert / 9, 20, 92, 100, 215, 258 © Elena Schweitzer / Cover, 15 © RetroClipArt
64 © AKaiser / 126, 127, 142, 143 © Mila Petkova

By **Clipart ETC** © 2011 University of South Florida, photos on pages:
26, 40, 60, 68, 108, 125, 153, 182, 192, 243, 245, 246, 251

All other illustrations used by permission © **Dover Publications, Inc.** on pages: cover, back cover,
1, 2, 3, 4, 5, 7, 8, 9, 10, 11, 12, 13, 14, 15, 16, 17, 18, 20, 21, 23, 24, 26, 29, 30, 32, 33, 34, 37, 38,
39, 40, 41, 42, 44, 46, 47, 48, 49, 50, 51, 52, 53, 54, 55, 56, 59, 60, 62, 63, 64, 67, 68, 70, 72, 73,
74, 75, 76, 78, 80, 82, 83, 84, 85, 86, 87, 88, 89, 91, 92, 93, 94, 95, 96, 99, 100, 102, 105, 106, 108,
110, 112, 114, 115, 116, 117, 118, 119, 121, 122, 124, 125, 126, 127, 128, 130, 131, 133, 135, 136,
137, 139, 140, 142, 143, 144, 145, 146, 147, 148, 151, 153, 154, 156, 159, 161, 162, 164, 166, 167,
168, 169, 171, 172, 175, 176, 179, 180, 182, 183, 185, 187, 188, 190, 192, 195, 197, 198, 201, 202,
204, 206, 209, 211, 212, 213, 214, 215, 217, 219, 220, 221, 223, 224, 226, 229, 230, 233, 235, 236,
239, 240, 243, 245, 246, 249, 250, 251, 252, 254, 261, 272

Other titles in this cookbook series:

Cooking with All Things Trader Joe's
by **Deana Gunn & Wona Miniati**
978-0-9799384-8-1

Cooking with Trader Joe's: Companion
by **Deana Gunn & Wona Miniati**
978-0-9799384-9-8

Cooking with Trader Joe's: Dinner's Done!
by **Deana Gunn & Wona Miniati**
978-0-9799384-3-6

Cooking with Trader Joe's: Lighten Up!
by **Susan Greeley, MS, RD**
978-0-9799384-6-7

Cooking with Trader Joe's: Skinny Dish!
by **Jennifer Reilly, RD**
978-0-9799384-7-4

Available everywhere books are sold.
Please visit us at

CookTJ.com